# The Legend of Dudleytown

*[Connecticut]*

## Solving Legends through
## Genealogical and Historical Research

## Gary P. Dudley

HERITAGE BOOKS
2008

# HERITAGE BOOKS

*AN IMPRINT OF HERITAGE BOOKS, INC.*


## Books, CDs, and more—Worldwide

For our listing of thousands of titles see our website
at
www.HeritageBooks.com


Published 2008 by
HERITAGE BOOKS, INC.
Publishing Division
100 Railroad Ave. #104
Westminster, Maryland 21157

International Standard Book Numbers
Paperbound: 978-0-7884-1778-8
Clothbound: 978-0-7884-7299-2

# Table of Contents

# Acknowledgments

A book like this is never done without some help. I do wish to express my gratitude to the following kind people:

**Nancy "Razz" Ziegler and Robin Boston Barron**. These wonderful folks belong to The Cosmic Society for Paranormal Investigation, and are also doing a book on Dudleytown. Now, I realize that they may be in competition with me, but we both had a hunger for facts, and we readily shared information, documents, and thoughts throughout the project(s). We are on opposite sides in the final conclusion, but God Bless them--some of the things within would not be there but for them. I have actually been able to call my competition friends. Good luck!

**Michael Gannet**. Curator of the Cornwall Historical Society. Mr. Gannett also assisted in sending vital records, pamphlets, and information I could not have gotten any other way. I wish to acknowledge this wonderful man and the Society for their selfless help.

**Catherine Siberling Pond**. An independent journalist who became interested in Dudleytown, and without knowing it contributed so much to my determination to finishing this book.

**Brian Maurisello and Jeff Ballenger**. Photo-journalists who also contributed to both my knowledge and my determination to "get the truth out." Thanks, guys!

**The members of Dark Entry Forest, Inc.** I really did not believe that any of these folk would help me. However, as the work progressed a few actually contacted me and shared a lot of the background and history of this organization, and Dudleytown itself. Words cannot express my appreciation to those that helped.

*The Legend of Dudleytown*

**Verna Gilson and the staff of the Litchfield Historical Society** contributed to the information on Mary Cheney Greeley

To the English Department of St. Francis Academy in San Antonio, along with Rev. George Wood, Nancy Van Evera, and Elsa Martinez for reading and re-reading this book and correcting my horrible spelling and other grammatical mistakes, my sincere appreciation.

There are also a few residents, and former residents, of Cornwall who do not wished to be named. You KNOW who you are. The documents, information, and other things you contributed to this book will be forever remembered. I understand your need for anonymity–may God Bless you.

To the thousands of visitors to my Dudleytown Website who have sent me words of encouragement and support, I will be forever grateful.

And finally

**Bonnie Jo Dudley** my wife and best friend for 29 years, and whom suffered through my obsession with this project and took the trip with me near the end. Rest in peace, my love. You earned it.

Gary P. Dudley
November 28, 2000

# Preface

One of my friends is a "ghost hunter." He always likes to tell me, upon seeing a place, a house, or even a picture........... "look closer, not all is as it seems!"

One day I did look closer. Guess what? He was right.

This little book has gone through three incarnations to arrive at the work you hold in your hands. As you will read, its genesis came about quite by accident. I am still in awe of the interest that the basic story–and the accompanying facts–has generated. I am also still surprised how easy it was to investigate it–85% of the work was done from my home in San Antonio, Texas. Any genealogist could have done it–even a beginner, as I was at the start. Being an avid history buff and history teacher made it even easier, but I still believe that anyone interested in genealogy, or history, could have found what I found. That no one had done it before shocks me!

The basic premise of this book is that with a little work anyone can solve historical mysteries if they want to (especially in the U.S.). This is particularly true with historical legends, which is what the Legend of Dudleytown is. We will begin by looking at what sparked my interest in this, then you will read the actual Legend of Dudleytown and the "historical" background to it. I will then show, step by step, the process I used to solve this mystery. Naturally, everything has a source–and I list them plainly as any good genealogist would do! From that, you may confirm anything I say for yourself. Along the way, you will find historical facts, history, and various odd bits of information that may or may not fascinate you. Near the end, we will look at Dudleytown today: who owns it; what has become of it; etc. Through that you will see what effect "legends" and ghosts stories can have on a community.

# DISCLAIMER

While some members of Dark Entry Forest, Inc., (DEF) did contribute facts and documents to me, THIS BOOK IS NOT CONDONED OR SUPPORTED BY THE DEF, AND THE INFORMATION CONTAINED HEREIN IS NOT TO BE CONSTRUED AS BEING SUBMITTED OR APPROVED BY THE CORPORATION.

The individuals who contributed to this book did so of their own free will and accord, and were not acting as representatives of DEF.

## The Legend of Dudleytown

You may ask why I, as a *history teacher*, chose to use genealogy *in addition* to history, to research this Legend. Wasn't history enough? You may be shocked to hear me say this-- but no, history was NOT enough. History is based *mostly* on SECONDARY sources. A secondary source is one that comes from documents *about* a subject. You take a little from this person's work, a little from that person's work. The documents may be (and usually are) written by people who were *not* actually present at the happening, or copies of documents that are made years after the original writer has died. Yes, PRIMARY documents (those *actually* written by participants, or actual records by the military or towns, all made at or near the time the event occurred), *are* used (and are becoming more so), but other sources *can* and usually do, seep in. Genealogy is (for the most part–and if it is done right) based almost *entirely* on primary sources. Genealogists are taught right from the beginning to research Census', Tax Records, Military, and State and Town Vital Records, along with Probate records, etc. to document their ancestor's existence. I would actually go so far as to say that genealogy is a *more reliable and exact science* than traditional history is. Let me give you a few examples from this work to show you what I mean:

HISTORY says: Mary Cheney Greeley was born in Cornwall (Dudleytown). This from the Cornwall Historical Society and Starr's *History of Cornwall.*

GENEALOGY says: She was born in Litchfield–the town over (and behind some hills) from Cornwall. This from the Litchfield Town Records, recorded at her birth.

HISTORY says: Mary Cheney Greeley committed suicide. This from ALL the Legend stories, *and* the Cornwall Historical Society.

GENEALOGY says: She died from Lung Disease, which she had for 20 years. This from her actual obituary.

HISTORY does *not* know how many Dudleytown brothers there were. This from virtually all accounts–both Legend and otherwise–of Dudleytown/Cornwall.

GENEALOGY shows that there were three of them. The rest of the Dudley's were from *different* branches of the family, not related to them, and they arrived at different times. This from various Town Records.

As you can see, going to the PRIMARY sources can really change things.

While the subject matter of this book may be unique (and some would say a little controversial), the *method* employed here is not. Historical research has been used at least twice in the past (that I am aware of) to look into supernatural things,[1] and genealogy has been used at least once before.[2] In all cases, once the background research is done, and done correctly, *what* happened usually will take second stage to the more interesting story of *why* it happened. That is what I have attempted here.

I am firmly aware that many of the readers of this book will

---

[1] Boyer, Paul and Stephen Nissenbaum, <u>Salem Possessed</u>, 1974, Harvard University Press, is an excellent look into the Salem Witch Trials using virtually every historical outlet available. Davidson, James West, and Mark H. Little <u>After the Fact, the Art of Historical Deduction</u>, 1992 McGraw Hill, is a look at a number of historical happenings using background material to give much fuller looks into history.

[2] Robinson, Enders A. <u>Salem Witchcraft and Hawthorne's "House of the Seven Gables"</u> 1992, Heritage Books

NOT be genealogists. My World Wide Web (internet) site has over 11,000 visits on it, and the site is just a little over a year old (as of this writing). Because I will promote this book through the site, I know that many will buy the book just to see the story and Legend in print. This book, you see, will be the *FIRST* book devoted entirely to the Legend. Therefore if something I write seems a little over-explained, that is the reason why. Who knows? Perhaps our noble hobby will gain a few more members!

In talking to other genealogists, I am aware that many families have oddities, mysteries, and assorted other weird stories attached to them. My family's mystery happened to be a huge one. Here, you will see how some of these mysteries can be accurately solved, and perhaps you will employ the same methods that I have used to delve into other areas of your research. The field is literally wide open!

Do not think that this is a book of pure debunking without any substance. In fact, debunking was one thing that I had never intended to do. The facts, *once I started noticing them, and then researched them*, just overwhelmed me. Knowing that people overlook facts in favor of sensationalism, I knew from the start that I just could not state the evidence–I would have to *show* it. Therefore, 95% of the facts are accompanied by sources.[3] As for history, the facts can be found in any history book, or with a simple combination of history and common sense thinking. A bibliography at the end will show most of the major volumes I turned to for most of the information. The genealogical data can be found at your

---

[3] A "source" to a genealogist is a listing of *where* they got the information. Town Vital Records, Probate records, and first hand documents (those written *at the time*), such as marriage and death certificates, etc are all reliable sources. A good genealogist will have a "source" for a person's birth, marriage, and death. If possible, they will verify all information with *two* "sources".

local library if it has a genealogical section, and local genealogical societies in your area will be a major source of help to you. You may also obtain help by going to your local Morman Family History Center, and asking the kind people there for help in your research. Additionally any large genealogical  web site may contain the information you need. My own genealogy site,  devoted to the D u d l e y  f a m i l y  n a m e,  i s  l o c a t e d  a t http://www.geocities.com/dudleyfam.

As stated, I have provided footnotes throughout showing were I have obtained my information. In the case of documents, the footnotes will state the sources for the documents. In some instances, I actually reproduce the document for you.  Yes, there is some conjecture in a few instances in the book. Some of these conjectures are based upon facts combined with common sense and circumstance, and in these instances I plainly state that.

The pictures and maps contained herein are original. The maps are *modified* from existing maps in the public domain. The modifications show various things *not* on the original ones, and were based upon historical documents. The photographs were taken by my friends Nancy "Razz" Ziegler and Robin Boston Barron, and are used with their permission.

This book is also unique in that it is the first research into the area in which members of Dark Entry Forest, Inc., have actually had an input. In view of this, you will find a disclaimer which states that while individual *members* have contributed, the corporation has not. You should not construe anything by this, as the DEF has *never* endorsed anything, and I never expected it to. The disclaimer speaks for itself. The areas that they contributed to are: History of Dudleytown, The Death of a Town, and DEF. For your information, they also supplied documents, some of which appear here, or are quoted from.

Should any new information be found after the printing of the book, my Dudleytown website is located at www.geocities.com/dtownfarce. Simply check there.

Before we go any farther though, let's take a brief look at what we will be discussing.

# Introduction

No place in Dudley Family history, or the history of Connecticut, has excited more interest than the little village of Dudleytown, which is technically a part of Cornwall Connecticut. The legend is one of the most well-known ghost stories in New England. It is featured in over 25 books, and has been the subject of an untold of number of magazine and newspaper articles. Every Halloween, some Connecticut newspaper will run a story on it. Actor Dan Ackroyd, in an 1983 Playboy article, called it "the most haunted place on earth."[4] Over 100 Web Sites on the World Wide Web have featured pages, some are entirely devoted to Dudleytown–and many of them have stated that the premiss for the movie *The Blair Witch Project* was inspired by Dudleytown. Actually, to get an indication as to just how widespread the Legend of Dudleytown is, log on to the internet, and do a search using the word "Dudleytown." You will be quite surprised. Some believe that H.P. Lovecraft's story "The Color out of Time" is based upon the Dudleytown legend, and that Thomas Tryon's novel Harvest Home is taken from the Legend. The story has all the makings of a really great horror story: historical figures, mysterious happenings, ghosts, a curse–but is it REALLY haunted, or just a "legend?" And you ask, how can a person *really* prove or disprove something like that? Well, I did, and so can you. Read on.

Let's take a trip!

We pile into our car and head for Cornwall, Connecticut. Coming into Cornwall, we look for Dark Entry Road–but we must look carefully, for while it does have a street sign, it can easily be missed. Finding the street, we park our car at the bottom of the hill in a small parking lot—the road from here is steep and up a paved

---

[4]Playboy Interview: Dan Ackroyd Playboy Magazine, August 1983, pgs 51-64. The quote is from pg 61.

road just large enough for one car (there is an occupied home on the road, and a Ranger Station is located on it), we run out of pavement about ½ of a mile on our journey. Here Dark Entry Road becomes a dirt trail--dangerous and impassible for cars.

The trail narrows, and becomes rocky. The trees become denser until only a little sunlight filters through. Then, off to the right side of the trail, we see a large hole in the ground. Walking towards it, we see the hole is rectangular, and lined with stones. We stand and look into what was once a cellar hole, that is, the cellar of a house that once stood here long ago.

Suddenly we hear the "hoot" of an owl and turn to see............nothing!

Welcome to DUDLEYTOWN, Connecticut's internationally infamous 'Village of the Damned!' Welcome to what is called "the scariest place in the USA." Welcome to the place of one of the most popular historical ghost stories in existence.

What are the ingredients of a good historical ghost story? Oh, a regular ghost story is easy–just make up anything you want, and if you are a good writer or story teller, you have it made! But a *historical* ghost story–that is something else again. They tend to be believed, and so some facts have to be true. Look at the Salem Witch Trials. There are still some who believe that there *really were* witches there! Yet, by just reading a good history of the trial, it can be readily seen that this was no more than a very unfortunate time of mass hysteria that was undoubtably caused by political intrigue, greed, and jealousy–very human elements.

Consider also the Amityville Horror. Once believed to be the true story of a haunting, there is now ample evidence to suggest that the entire affair was a fraud.

But we all *love* a good ghost story–and better yet one that might be ***true!*** Towns all over the U.S. have houses that people swear are haunted–and the residents of the area can tell you the story behind them, too! The stories are based upon fact–you can actually check the newspapers. Urban Legends come from the same stuff–things that actually happened, but are so embellished that sometimes separating fact from fiction takes a true detective.

Such is the Legend of Dudleytown, Connecticut. A town born out of a land auction, worked by our forefathers, and failed. A victim of the Westward Expansion and rocky soil. Simply that.

So what made Dudleytown so famous? Easy. An isolated set of forgotten buildings, seven unfortunate happenings within a 10 mile radius, one woman who supposedly went insane, and one book article in 1938. That is all it took.

First, the book, They Found A Way, written in 1938, gave it an historical background. A curse from England! What could be better? Second, the book took the unfortunate things that *did* happen there and gave them a supernatural slant. The story ended with the town deserted and no one daring to go there. Dates and names abounded–famous ones, too. It all looked so very good.

Other magazines, tabloids (most notably, the National Enquirer) and books picked up on it, and the story grew bigger. Lastly, the world's most noted "Psychic Investigators" and "Demonologists" Ed and Lorraine Warren, wrote a chapter in their book "Ghost Hunters" about it. Dudleytown is now famous throughout the nation and the Internet. Books are plentyfull, pictures of "ghost lights" abound, and stories continue to come forth from this little hill—and millions of people believe them.

There is only ONE small problem.

Nobody checked the facts.

That, kind reader, is what we are going to do here. We will look at the background, dates, deaths, history, and everything else connected to this town. And I did it all with only what I know about genealogy and history. You can too!

So let's begin!

# Prelude
### A prophecy

"On the Connecticut Hills, overlooking the valley of Housatonic near Cornwall Bridge, there is an elevation of abandoned farm land, pasture and forest several thousand acres in area. From the bare tops of this elevation there are lovely views of the rugged hills and wooded valleys of the Berkshire or Taconic range. There are trout in the streams, partridges in the woods, and berries in the fields. There are forgotten roads and crumbling walls of other days. A row of apple trees buried in the woods, a mass of lilac blooms among the brambles, give the wayfarer sudden pause.... *"Here someone lived."*

"This countryside was settled before the Revolution, and prosperous farming was possible up to the Civil War. The forest had been so recently cut away that there was still great wealth in the soil, and the crops were bounteous. There was a thriving community known as *DUDLEYTOWN*, from which twelve wagon loads of parents and children were wont to drive down Agag Hill to church.

Depletion of the soil rapidly cames, industries changed, the old town was deserted; a new forest has since then grown up where once were hayfield, pasture, and roadside. The old stone walls now serve as wondrous Roman roads for red squirrel and chipmunk, or as chance resting places for the passerby. The forest is coming back to its own;...*but if it is not protected, it will surely be sacrificed, as many another forest of New England has been sacrificed shortsightedly, without regard to the many years which have gone to its making, or its value to the country-side."*

—Dr. William Cogswell Clarke.
Written in 1924, at the time of
the incorporation of Dark

# GENESIS

*"I call it 'the noble hobby', and it is! Here you will find your roots, both good and bad"[5]*

I have always loved history. Since the earliest times that I can remember, I was always good in this subject. In school I rarely had to study for a history test because everything about history that I read or was taught stayed in my mind so well that I could recall the facts quickly. Even in High School, I received a B without even trying. I loved it! I also recall that at a tender age I would always listen with interest when my family would talk about relatives I had not met, or those that had died. I heard about genealogy–the study of one's ancestors–and thought that would be a very interesting hobby, never believing that I would ever get the chance to research my family.

I was married in 1970, joined the Air Force in 1974, and raised our three children partly overseas, and partly in the United States. I was on my last overseas tour in Alaska when everything came together, and I began a lifelong investigation into the ancestry of my family. In 1990, I decided to join the Masons. I was given a family bible by my Masonic lodge in Alaska. It was a common gift for the lodge to give a newly "raised" Master Mason, and while I had a few other family Bibles, I decided to go ahead and fill in the "Family Record" section in the new one. I quickly found out that I did not have enough information to go back three generations, and began calling my family for further information. I contacted just about every living relative (many that I had never met) and gleaned a lot of information. One call led me to my Uncle Clifford in Connecticut, who asked me "Do you know about our haunted town–Dudleytown?" I didn't, so he mailed me a small booklet about it. I read the little book, and thought it was quite fascinating.

---

[5]From an introduction to one of my books, as yet unpublished.

2

## The Legend of Dudleytown

It spoke of murders, ghosts, and things with hoofed feet, in a little Connecticut town with my family name! But, I put it aside for a while, as the research on the family had taken a serious turn—I was HOOKED on genealogy! My formative years as a genealogist were between 1990-1992. I was learning how to do research, bought a program to do it on my computer, and learned about sources. As I look back on it now, I see that it was also about that time that my wife began referring to our computer as my "square headed girlfriend."

I returned to the "lower 48" (Alaskan slang for the contiguous United States) in 1992, retired from the Air Force in 1994, and became a History Teacher at St. Francis Academy, a Catholic High School for girls here in San Antonio. The school wanted a web page, so I learned all about HTML[6] and put one up for them. It attracted attention, and as I learned more about the World Wide Web I found hundreds of genealogical pages on it. It only took me two hours to design a web site for my family and put it up. At first, I only wanted to see if anyone was interested in the Dudley family name. It exceeded my wildest expectation, and that page I first put up has grown into one of the largest single-surname sites on the web. But I digress.

One slow afternoon, I decided to add a one page short story about Dudleytown. Did anyone else believe it was haunted? The answer was quick in coming; in one month I had over 200 email letters about that one small page, and most of it agreed that the town was haunted. Priding myself on accuracy, I began to consider doing a little research on it. Actually, I though it would be fun—a genuine haunted town in the family! Great!

---

[6]HTML refers to Hyper Text Markup Language—the computer language that Internet pages are written in.

## The Legend of Dudleytown

In 1993, I went to seminary to further my desire to become a Traditional Episcopal Priest, and wanting something to read on the bus, I picked up a copy of <u>Ghost Hunters</u> by Ed and Lorraine Warren, two well known "demonologists." (the book is now out of print, but can still be found in libraries). It contained a story called "The Haunted Village," all about Dudleytown. Wow! More documentation! This was going to be fun. Or so I thought.

As time went on, I collected more versions of the Dudleytown story through various books, magazines, and through the web page (which had grown from one page to 10). Many people sent me newspaper articles about it. Each contained a slightly different version of the Legend, the background to it, and a little "history" of the town, insights, and other things. I started a file with the information and it became quite large very quickly.

I had to admit I *was* a little bothered by some of the differences in the various versions of the Legend. While a little differentiation in stories, even in history books, is expected due to different authors' outlooks, some basic foundations were so different that they caught my eye. This was especially true in the genealogical data that most of the stories provided to give it a basic historical foundation. I knew something might be wrong, but it took my teaching job to show me what that something was.

The first real proof that something was amiss came one day in the U.S. History class I teach. The day's lesson was the French and Indian War. You will shortly read that the legend states that three (or four, depending on which version of the legend you read) Dudleytown brothers were returning from the French and Indian War in 1747, and shortly thereafter founded Dudleytown. What was wrong with that? To those who do not remember their history, nothing is wrong! (and I am ashamed to admit that I missed it too) Well, the lesson went like this:

4

## The Legend of Dudleytown

"Ok class, what were the dates of the French and Indian War?"

"1754 to 1763, Mr. Dudley."

I paused. Wait a minute, how could the Dudleytown brothers be returning from a war *that hadn't even started yet?*

That one little discovery led me to decide to use genealogical research methods, combined with good, old fashioned history, to dig into this well-known legend and find out what really happened. I had a bad feeling that I would find more inaccuracies. I was right.

I started to organize the data I had collected and compared it to basic history. My happiness at finding a "haunted" village in the family soon turned to bewilderment and then into anger. How could so many of these inaccuracies been missed by so many "professional" authors? I started making lists of what I would research first. You are reading the outcome.

Before we can go any farther, however, it now becomes necessary lay down a little background, both historically and mythically. I try to inspire (if that is humanly possible with teenagers) my girls to study history by telling them "You can't know where you are if you don't know were you've been."

So here we go! Buckle your historical seatbelts, put on your thinking caps, and come with me "to those thrilling days of yesteryear."

Our story will begin in England.

# The Family Behind the Legend, Part 1

*"..the thing abut folklore is that the truth of the matter is NOT important, the existence of the story is the important thing."*[7]

In the normal course of researching my family name, I obviously looked into its beginnings. San Antonio has a fairly good library with a genealogical section, but NO genealogical library or research center is set up to research one single surname (last name). I did have to "special order," through the libraries inter-library loan, a few books, and I also bought one or two that I knew I would be using again and again. Most genealogists will always tell you that they are continually researching the origins of their family, for it's a never ending job. Here is what I have found thus far on the surname Dudley.

The Dudley name is very old. According to Dean Dudley, author of the monumental (but often confusing) History of the Dudley Family,[8] (and other authors) a Saxon man by the name of Dudd (or Dudde) died in 725 A.D. His title was "Duke of Mercia,"and he owned the land that eventually became the site of Dudley Castle. Now, as an old English word for "land" or "field" was "leigh" or "lay," it was natural to call the land "Dudd's leigh," and shorten it to--you guessed it--Dudley. When John de Sutton took over the land, he was called "Sir John de Sutton, Lord Dudley." He was a "Sir" because he was a Knight. "de Sutton" to designate his origin, and "Lord Dudley" to designate his

---

[7]Myers, Arthur "Is the Ghost Village of Dudleytown Really Haunted?" from A Ghosthunters's Guide., 198?, Chicago, Contemporary Books. The quote is from an interview with William DeVoti, Page 57.

[8]Dudley, Dean History of the Dudley Family, Vol 1, No.1, 1886, Salem Mass. Reprint, Higginson Books, pg 36

Barony--the land of Dudd's leigh.

Now it gets a little confusing--please try to follow.

John Sutton married Isabel de Charlton (daughter of John de Charlton) and John died in 1359. Now, THEIR children kept the name Sutton until about 1420. In the meantime, they went on to hold the castle and eventually changed their name to "de Dudley" and then just "Dudley" in said year 1420. They became known as the "Lords of Dudley" or "Barons of Dudley." They are also known as the "second house."[9]

SECOND house? Well (I told you it gets complicated), after John died Isabel married one Richard de Dudley in 1361. THEIR children immediately assumed the name Dudley, and became the FIRST house (simply because they took the name first). Now--these Dudley's are known as the CLOPTON Dudley's, because, although it is not well documented, Thomas de Dudley, one of Richard's sons, settled in Clopton, England and became Lord of Clopton manor. This was because the OTHER Dudleys had the castle and the land that would eventually be called the town of Dudley, England. See, I told you it's a little boggling.

The other line--those that held the castle and took the name latter--are known as the SUTTON Dudley's.

We now have TWO lines of Dudley's (springing from the same mother, but different fathers) producing offspring.

ALL DUDLEY'S TODAY COME FROM THE ABOVE HISTORY. It is the Second house, the Sutton Dudley's, that we are

---

[9]Adlaird, George The Sutton Dudley's of England 1862, now published by the Genealogical Publishing House.

concerned with here.

One of John Sutton's sons was named Edmund.

*We now we depart from the world of TRUE genealogy, and are magically transported to:*

**The EDMUND DUDLEY Story**.

This is where the Legend of Dudleytown supposedly starts, and is cited as the foundation of all the "curse" stories. Note that there are two versions of the story. Unfortunately, as I have stated, there are two or more versions to everything at Dudleytown.

*Please note that what follows below is the genealogy and the story of the LEGEND, NOT the TRUE genealogy, or story, that REALLY happened. That you will find later on. Also note that NONE of the books these "histories" come from state where they got their information!*

# Version One[10]

In 1510 Edmund Dudley was beheaded for plotting to overthrow the King of England (we are not told why, but details *never* matter in these things). It was then, some conjecture, a curse was placed upon him and his kin. Or maybe not (this version appears slightly different in each source). His son, John Dudley, Duke of Northumberland, also tried to take the throne of England by marrying HIS son, Guilford Dudley, to one Lady Jane Grey, and

---

[10] This is the most common version, and is paraphrased from the following books, all referenced in the bibliography at the end: They Found a Way; Legendary Connecticut; Folk Tales of Connecticut.

placed her on the throne of England. She lasts there nine days before being displaced by her cousin Mary Tudor. Failing to accomplish their goal, all three lost their heads. Right after this, Johns OTHER son (not named) returned from France with the plague. It killed thousands--including him. But wait, John had ANOTHER son, and he meant to keep his head. His name was Robert, Earl of Leicester, and he decided to leave England forever. Now, Robert had a son, William Dudley, who came to America in 1630. He had sons, and here is where our Legend starts....

# Version Two[11]

In this version, Thomas Dudley of the Massachusetts Bay Company (later to be Governor Thomas Dudley of the Colony of Massachusetts) is related to Edmund (above) and is an Uncle to *four* Dudley Brothers who discover the area of Dudleytown and settle it. The brothers are: Abijah, Bavzillai (*sic*); Gideon; and Abviel (*sic*). They founded Dudleytown in 1632.

In this story, Governor Dudley is a horrible man, and has everyone who is not Puritan put to death. One of the many men he had executed cursed "not only the deputy governor, but the entire area of Dudleytown, damning it forever. After serving four different terms as full governor, a curious fate befell Thomas Dudley-he was found hacked to death in the area that would later come to be known as Dudleytown." The murderer is never found, and this is where our Legend starts..........

---

[11]This version ONLY appears in: Warren, Ed and Lorraine with Robert David Chase, Ghost Hunters, 1989, St. Martin's Paperbacks, pgs 173-182. In fact, the *entire* Warren story of Dudleytown differs from the others so much that most Dudleytown researchers discount their version entirely.

You are about to read THE LEGEND OF DUDLEYTOWN. The version you will read is a combination of all the different variations that have been printed to ensure you get a good mix of all the different versions. The only thing I have done that is different is to put it into story form, and attempted to write it as if you were reading a book full of ghost stories and this is one of them. Should you not like it, feel free to pick up a copy of any of the others. In fact, I suggest you do so to get the feel of the different versions.

Note that ONE of the above versions of the genealogies (histories) just presented will accompany the legend, usually at the beginning of the story.

Knowing this, don't worry about the genealogy and history for a few moments. Sit back, get comfortable, and turn down the lights........get ready for a good old-fashioned ghost story!

# The Legend of Dudleytown

The owls--those cursed owls, hooting all night long--most of the time during the day, too. The town is never really sunny; there is always a haze. It's mainly because of the location, completely surrounded as it is by hills. The little town is next to Cornwall and has two entrances--though you will have to look hard for them. One is called Dudleytown Road and the other by the ominous name of Dark Entry. It's deserted now except for the occasional teenagers out for a thrill, or maybe a few Satanists wanting to cast their spells in a "real" haunted town. If a town is what you can still call it. There are a few stone foundations and what is left of a chimney here or there. And, of course, there's the "curse." Should you wander out there some day, it will be the owls that will really bother you--those cursed owls!

A long time ago, in 1747, the first Dudleys arrived there, and settled this area. First it was Abiel and Barzillai, brothers returning from the French and Indian wars, and later Gideon and Abijah came to the town and settled. Martin and LaFayette Dudley arrived later. The town didn't have a name then, but as the Dudley's quickly became involved with the building of the town and it's affairs, the village adopted the name of "Dudleytown." The other folks: the Carters, the Andrews, Deacon Porter, and the Pattersons all agreed. Some, though, wanted to call it "Owlsbury." And for good reason--those cursed owls! Hooting day and night!

The work on building Dudleytown was very tedious. Trees-- thick trees--were everywhere and had to be felled. The wood was used to build the houses at first; later the houses would be made of stone. The wood was later used to make charcoal for the nearby iron works. Rocks and large stones were located where trees weren't, and these had to be moved also--back breaking work! But people were rugged in those days, and the town prospered. By 1800, the little town had its own meeting house and improved roads named Dudleytown Road and Dark Entry road. Dark Entry was named that because the tall trees on the road made the entire passage on it very dim, even at noon. There were a few others, but these were the main roads--the ones that would appear on maps. But the expansion, and the town itself, would never make it through the Civil War. Something in the area was amiss and everyone knew it. Some said it was jinxed, some blamed it on a curse. Maybe it was the owls-- those cursed owls!

John Andrews then built a wall out of stone; some say it was he who finally inspired people to begin building with stone. He sure did like that wall! When done, he stepped back and inspected it. "This, if nothing else, will last" he said.

Then came the bad times......

Some say it started with Abiel. Oh, he lived long enough. He outlived the other Dudley's, but he seemed to go feeble-minded. Mad, in fact, though somewhat harmless. He kept shouting about "hoofed creatures" and such. What is sad is that though his family lent their name to the town, "Old Biel," as they called him, died as a town charge--a pauper, and totally insane. So, the curse of the Dudley family had started. Would it end?

Most people believe that it was Nathaniel Carter that set the "Dudley Curse" working on the rest of the town. He bought the house that Abiel Dudley had lived in. Abiel lost it when he became a town charge; it was said that Barzillai sold it in 1759 to pay for his debts.

Things never did seem to go right for Nathaniel any more. Especially when, after all the hardship they caused old Abiel, they up and moved out of Dudleytown in 1763, and went to live near

Binghamton, New York. What was odd is that while the whole family moved, their 13 year old son Nathan seemed to have been left behind in Dudleytown! It turns out that he was the lucky one.

In October of 1764, the door of the new Carter home burst open, and the Indians attacked. They split Mother Carter's head open with a tomahawk, bashed baby Carter's brains out against a wall, burned the cabin, and took the three living children (two daughters and a son) captive. Nathaniel himself was scalped immediately upon his return from a hunting trip. The children were never seen again....

Nathaniel's brother Adoniram fared no better, when in 1774 six members of his family (some sources say his wife and only child) died from a mysterious and unknown epidemic.

Back in Dudleytown, in 1792 Gershon Hollister was found murdered at William Tanner's home. It generated a long investigation and quite a scandal. He was found innocent, but Tanner was never quite right after that. He died later, totally insane, and some say he would occasionally cry out about "demons" and other creatures.

One of Dudleytown's most famous men was General Herman Swift, who was an aid to General George Washington, Commander of the Continental Army and soon to be President. One stormy afternoon his wife Sarah was struck in the head by lightning and killed instantly, right on her front porch while he was off with General Washington. When he returned to learn of Sarah's death an odd thing happened; this great General whom had seen many battles began to lose his mind.

In 1813 another unexplained epidemic struck the little town, this time taking scores of people, including half of the Jones' family.

Then there's the story of Horace "go west, young man, go west" Greeley. He married Mary Cheney, who was born and raised in Dudleytown. She followed her husband, of course, and supported him even through his campaign for the Presidency. Now, if a lagging campaign doesn't get one stressed out, figure out what would happen to a person who, one week before the election, finds that his wife, late of Dudleytown, decided to climb up on a chair and jump--with only a rope around her neck to stop her! The people of Dudleytown mourned her loss--those of them that were left. They mourned, that is, when they weren't cursing those owls!

More and more, year after year, crops failed, the unexplained deaths continued; farm animals came up missing. Families began leaving, and by 1880 Dudleytown was all but a ghost town. Only one resident remained of note in the later years of the 1800's--John Brophy.

Brophy moved there because he liked the solitude. He figured it was only a short walk down Dark Entry Road to the nearby town, and he could raise his sheep with his two sons and his wife. The only thing he really didn't like was the constant hooting of the owls--those cursed owls! It did not take long before things started going amiss. First, both his sons disappeared. Then his sheep began to disappear--where to? Who knows! His wife died of unknown causes, but he was Irish! He would stick it out!

The nearby town villagers began to notice Brophy coming into town with torn clothes. He had a wild look in his eyes, and wouldn't talk to anyone. He did mutter, though. Those that heard the muttering said it was something about "demons" and things with hoofed feet. It must have been lonely for him up there--with only the owls to keep him company on those walks down Dark Entry Road--very lonely. Then, one very dark night, his house burned to the ground. The people from the town tried to help--but they couldn't. They didn't find Brophy that night, not his body or anything. And they never did find him--he had completely disappeared.

Dudleytown remained empty until the 1920's, when a New York Pathologist--one Dr. William Clark, built a summer home there. Things were quiet for a time. Then, one day, the good doctor was called to New York on business, and though his wife pleaded with him not to go, he left immediately. After a few days he returned, his business completed, expecting to find his wife waiting for him at the train station--but she wasn't there. He traveled up Dark Entry Road with the cursed owls hooting the entire distance to his home in what was left of Dudleytown. As he entered his house he called out to his wife only to be answered by a low cackling! He found his wife upstairs--laughing uncontrollably, totally insane!

What happened while he was gone? No one knows. He left, and never returned. Dudleytown has been deserted ever since.

Time moves forward, to the 1950's. A teenage boy comes stumbling into the local Police station, yelling about how his girlfriend and he was chased down Dark Entry Road by something with hoofed feet and green eyes. More stories start to come in.....and Dudleytown is finally removed from the Connecticut maps--for safety!

Later, in the 1980's, a Television crew decide to go to Dudleytown to film a Halloween story. They load up their vans with the equipment, and proceed up Dark Entry Road, laughing and telling stories to set the mood. The attractive Anchorwoman is jovial too! What fun! They arrive at the town, get ready to shoot--- but suddenly their cameras don't work! Try as they might, nothing seems to want to cooperate with them, except the owls. Those cursed owls! Hooting constantly!

So they loaded up and returned to the studio. Their producer is angry, why no story? He is told that the cameras would not work. The producer picks one up, plugs it in and aims it at the crew--and turns it on. It works just fine.

By now the "Curse of Dudleytown" is famous. There are articles in magazines, stories in history books about the area, and even the most famous Ghost Hunters in America have a story about it in one of their books. It is now called "the most Haunted Place in New England!" With that came the Paranormal Societies and Investigators, all wanting a "crack" at Dudleytown to solve the mystery.

In the 1990's one group arrives, about 16 of them, with equipment and cameras. They are guided by two investigators and are shown the area–particularly the "dead zones" and the "Vortex."[12] Upon entering the Vortex, the male guides knees begin to quake, his body shivers, and he drops to the ground, yelling "Oh, this place is EVIL, get me out!" They leave the Vortex, and he regaines his composure. They take many photographs that evening, but nothing else happens--until they have the pictures developed. Strange lights appear in them, and mists.

What had they REALLY met with?

Stories do continue about the town, however. Stories about Satan Worshipers, and motorcycle gangs who hold strange rites. In addition, the usual tales of lovers who are scarred out of their wits when they "park" there, being attacked by "demons", things with

---

[12]We will examine the Vortex in a later chapter.

16

hoofed feet and green eyes! UFO's have been seen there, and the Indian Burial Ground nearby. A bigfoot-like creature has been seen--and other oddities that no one can explain.

One thing they all mentioned, though, was the stone wall. John Andrews had said that wall would endure, though, didn't he? And, of course, the constant hooting of the owls--those cursed, cursed owls!

# The Family Behind the Legend, Part 2

*"I don't care how many 'facts' you have, the curse came through the Dudley's, I don't know how, but it just HAS to be!"*[13]

The story sounded really good, didn't it? You may have even read accounts in magazines and books about it. Everybody thinks it's haunted--but is it?

Oh, I *really* wanted it to be! A *genuine* haunted town in my families history! Wow!

Then, just like the Legend, the bad times came.

As I have previously stated, the first hint that something was amiss came one day in my U. S. History class. But as I began my research into the Legend, I found many, many more inaccuracies. You see, the sensational accounts were not the only accounts. As a teacher, I know that history usually records only the event–not necessarily *why* or *how* the event came about. One thing I always tell my students is that history, *real* history, always has a *foundation*. In other words, *something* happens because *something else* happened to *cause* it. So, if you know the facts concerning a occurrence, you can usually find out what REALLY happened. In Dudleytown's case, the situation WAS historical. We have the dates, names, and places for what had supposedly happened there. So lets move on to our first concern. As you will see, maybe Dudleytown was just never meant to be.

Lets start with the genealogy of Dudleytown. Is the "curse"

---

[13]From an Email critical of my research. Name withheld.

story of the people behind Dudleytown true?

To begin any historical or genealogical investigation you have to start by looking at what you have been TOLD. First, and foremost--the curse came through the Dudley line. But what Dudley line are we talking about? We are given *two* different genealogies to work with depending on who is telling the story---and as I am a genealogist, I think the facts that are needed to either prove or disprove either of them are readily available. And, unfortunately, both versions of the "curse," I found, are IMPOSSIBLE!

I began my research by delving into my expanding database of Dudley's that I had collected and simply brought the vital information up. I then compared it to historical texts and books, and found that both agreed with each other. The history, then, of the *principals* (the people involved) and the *area* of the "curse" were well known and documented.

Lets start by a look at common history in comparison to the first of the "versions" of the genealogy presented in part one. We will begin with our old friend Edmund Dudley.

Edmund Dudley (1462-1510)[14] was financial advisor (his official title was "Exchequer") to King Henry VII. Edmund was an expert on finances, and even wrote books on it. Henry needed Edmund's expertise, and got it. Unfortunately, Henry was not a nice man. He was rich, and wanted to be richer, and used Edmund's advice to rape the English economy. When Henry VII died, Henry VIII came to the throne, and the people wanted revenge. Whom

---

[14]Any good history book about the Tudor Kings and Queens will do for confirmation about Edmund. A short version of the information can be found in the Encyclopedia Britannica. Note that almost all of the historical data is very easy to check.

should Henry VIII offer them? The only people that the citizens would know was at least partially responsible—Edmund Dudley and his associate, Mr. Epson. They were confined to the famous Tower of London. While there, Edmund wrote a short book advising Henry how to financially manage England–which Henry used till the day he died! Edmund's head rolled from his body on August 18, 1510. Did Henry VIII really believe it was Edmund's fault that England was raped? No. In most cases of this type, the traitor's land, title, and everything else he owned would be stripped of him. In Edmunds case, this did *not* happen. Edmund was simply a scapegoat–Edmund knew it, Henry VIII knew it, and most historians today acknowledge it. There was *never* any indication of a curse being put on Edmund Dudley. At least historically.

Let us move on.

One of Edmund's sons was named John Dudley, who became the Duke of Northumberland. Here history gets a little confusing, so try to follow. When Henry VIII died, his only son Edward became King Edward the Sixth. However, he was so young that an advisor had to be appointed, and at first the position fell to the Duke of Somerset. To make a long story short, he was later replaced by John Dudley, Duke of Northumberland. When it appeared that Edward had a short time to live, most of England feared that Edward's sister, Mary Tudor, would come to the throne and make the Roman Catholic religion England's religion, and cause a bloody civil war. John Dudley and Henry Grey, the Duke of Suffolk, had a plan—have John's son Guilford marry Henry's daughter Jane, and place Jane on the throne of England before Mary had a chance to claim it (Jane was Mary's cousin, so there *was* some validity to it–although Mary was rightfully the successor).

Henry died, and John's plan went into action, and Jane Grey Dudley became Queen of England—for *nine* days. Mary charged

Jane with usurping the throne, took power, and Guilford, John, Jane's father and Jane herself all lost their heads. (and yes, Mary sent so many people to both the stake and headman's block that history names her "Bloody Mary")

John, however, had other sons, enumerated below:[15]

Henry. He died young.
Thomas. He died young.
John. He married, but had no children.
Ambrose. The famous Earl of Warwick. He married three times, but no children.
Henry. No children.
Charles. He died young.

And then there is the most famous of John's sons-- Robert Dudley, who was the Earl of Leicester.[16]

Robert Dudley was born 24 June 1532. He is one of histories most colorful characters, and was a lifelong "favorite" of Queen Elizabeth.[17] He married two times that are known, and had

---

[15]Dean Dudley, Vol. 1, and Adlaird both present an identical list. In addition, since this family was considered royalty (even if for a few days), their pedigree is plainly stated in any number of books on the Kings and Queens (especially the Tudor's) of England.

[16]As you can not study Queen Elizabeth I without a legion of references to Robert, information on him was quite easy to find. The most recent (and complete) is Alison Weir's Life of Elizabeth I, 1998, Balantine Books.

[17]Just what his relationship was with the Queen, no one knows. It is generally accepted that he had an affair with her, but history can not confirm it.

an unacknowledged marriage to Lady Douglas Sheffeld. His first marriage was to Amy Robsart, which produced no children. His affair (at least) with Lady Douglas occurred next, and this produced a son, Robert.[18] His third (or second legitimate) marriage was to Letitia (Lettice) Knollys, widow of Walter Deveroux, the Earl of Essex. This brought into the marriage a stepson, Robert Deveroux, who became Earl of Essex, inheriting the title from his father Walter. Robert Dudley never acknowledged his step son, even in his will. As for his illegitimate son Sir Robert Dudley, he called him his "base son", and didn't mention him in his will either. Letitia finally gave him a legitimate son, also named Robert, but he died before his first birthday.

Robert Dudley, Earl of Leicester, never left England. He died in Warwick England on 4 September 1588, and was buried there. Upon his death, his illegitimate son Sir Robert petitioned for his fathers' property and rights, but was refused. Sir Robert left his wife and 4 daughters in England (well cared for) and took his mistress Elizabeth Southwell (disguised as a boy) and went to Italy. Because of the lingering antagonistic attitudes between the Church of England and the Roman Catholic Church, it was easy for Sir Robert to obtain a dispensation from the Pope for a divorce, and he married his mistress there and had 13 children.

The Italians loved Sir Robert, and he became very wealthy. He carried the title "Duke of Northumberland," but wether he assumed that title or the Pope granted it to him is still a mystery. One source says it was granted him by "the (Holy Roman Empire) Emperor." In 1613 he bought an estate of the Rucellai family in the Parish of St. Pancras. He is credited for building the Port of

---

[18]Most History and Genealogy books differentiate father Robert from son Robert by naming the son "Sir Robert." We will follow that method.

Leghorn, inventing "several methods for improving ships," and drawing a large number of English merchants into the port of Leghorn. He died in Florence in September 1649, a well respected man. Upon his death, his son Charles took the title "Duke of Northumberland." Sir Robert's wife Elizabeth was styled "Duchess Dudley," and there is a monument to her in the church of St. Pancratius in Florence.

Sir Robert's children were:[19]
>  1. Cosmo. He died young.
>  2. Charles (a.k.a. Carlo). He married Mary Magdalen, daughter of the Duke of Rhoanet, and had five children. Charles died in Florence. Of the five children of Charles, two were boys: Robert, who renounced his dukedom to his brother. He became chamberlain to Queen Maria Christiana of Sweden, who lived in Rome at the time. Anthony, the other son, seems to have taken his Uncle Anthony's position of Canon of the Cathedral of the Vatican at his Uncle's death. No children.
>  3. Ambrose. No information is known. Is said to have died in Florence.
>  4. Anthony. A Priest, Canon of the Cathedral of the Vatican. No children.
>  5. Ferdinand. Was a Dominican Friar. No children.
>  6. Henry. Styled "Earl of Warwick." No information known. Said to have died in Florence.
>  7. An unnamed son, died in infancy.
>  8. Anna. Buried at St. Pancreas Church in 1629.
>  9. Mary

---

[19]This information comes from Dudley, Dean <u>History of the Dudley Family</u>, Vol 2, No.8, 1893, Salem Mass. Higginson Books reprint, pages 847-850.

10. Teresa. Married the Earl of Carpegna.
11. An unnamed Daughter whom married the Prince of Pombino.
12. Another unnamed Daughter whom married the Marquis Chivola.
13. Another Daughter, married the Duke of Casteleaon del Lago.

As you will see, when Sir Robert, ONLY living son of Robert Dudley, Earl of Leicester, bought his estate in Italy, William Dudley, ancestor of the Dudleytown brothers, who was born September 11, 1605, *was already five years old.*[20]

That finishes our (very) short look at history and the first version of the "curse" genealogy. Now lets look at the second version, which deals with Governor Thomas Dudley.

I wish to state before we begin that Version Two of the "curse" genealogy is ONLY found in Ed and Lorraine Warren's book Ghost Hunters. It is found nowhere else. The reason I will cover this version is simply because of their popularity and the coverage the media has given them. They have sold millions of books, and have had a lot of television coverage, and it is quite possible that their readers have believed their statements at face value.

As a reminder to you, the Warren's state that Dudleytown brothers line of descent extends to (Governor) Thomas Dudley of the Massachusetts Bay Company as their uncle, and that Governor

---

[20]So how did anyone link William to Robert? See the appendix.

Dudley was descended from Edmund Dudley.[21]

First, the ancestry of Governor Thomas Dudley is lost forever. No one knows it. The farthest back it can be traced is to his father, Captain Roger Dudley's marriage in Bedfordshire, England. Theories abound in the Genealogical World (as there are literally *thousands* of his descendants alive today), and the debate over the lineage has gone on for decades.[22] Very famous and scholarly genealogists have attempted to complete the pedigree, but none have been successful. Part of the problem has been that thousands of Parishes were destroyed during Cromwell's time, and along with them their records. Additionally, political intrigue seems to have followed this branch of the Dudley family, with problems to numerous to list. However, none of investigators into the pedigree of Governor Dudley has ever linked the him to Edmund Dudley. NONE.

One thing is certain: the lineage from Governor Thomas, and the line for William Dudley, from whence came the Dudleytown brothers, are two entirely different lines of the family. They are not connected. But history will serve our cause better here.

Governor Thomas Dudley died 31 July, 1653 in Roxbury, Massachusetts[23] (hundreds of miles from Dudleytown). He died of natural causes–not "hacked to death." Dudleytown was founded in 1747, 94 *years later* (and this is if we agree on the accepted

---

[21]Warren, pg 175.

[22]The debate over Gov. Dudley's ancestry continues to this day. It is said that the New England Historical Society has on-going research into it.

[23]Sources are to numerous to cite, any history book will do.

founding date of the town). When the Dudleytown brothers were born, Governor Thomas *had been dead 53 years*. Since Governor Dudley's life has been so well documented, the only question that should be asked is: "who made this story up?"

There are more problems with this theory. NO one has been able to say WHEN such curse would have been placed on them, or, who did it (except the Warrens). Should we accept either of the versions, the ONLY unfortunate happenings to the Dudleys' (especially to those in theory number one--where we have all the beheading's) are political things that THEY brought about themselves! Any research into the history of England at that time will reveal that political intrigue was the norm--not the exception. If a curse had been involved, it should have been readily apparent by strange happenings or sudden deaths. None are present.

As a final act of providing proof of their being no connection to, or between, any of the above principals in our story, allow me to set forth the birth and death dates of all of them.

Edmund Dudley      1462-1510  He is our foundation.

Robert Dudley      24 June 1532 - 4 September 1588
                   The Earl of Leicester. The "curse" pivot.

Sir Robert         1573 - September 1649    He is the ONLY
                   person that could provide  male offspring to
                   carry any   "curse." His 1st male child was
                   born about 1610 in Italy, AFTER the birth of
                   William, below.

Governor Thomas
Dudley                   Baptized 12 October 1576, died 31 July 1653

William Dudley    11 September 1608 - ? The first ancestor of
the Dudleytown Brothers to arrive in
America. Note that William was born 20 years
AFTER the death of the Earl of Leicester.

To have been connected to Robert Dudley, Earl of Leicester,
William Dudley and Governor Thomas Dudley would either have
HAD to have been sons of the Earl of Leicester, OR sons of Sir
Robert, the Earl's only living son. They were not. As we can see,
ALL of them were CONTEMPORARIES of each other, not related
at all.

Case closed.

So far, all of the above is simple history. Anyone can research it
with minimal time. I did the entire process within two weeks,
starting from scratch.

Satisfied that the beginnings of the "curse" were bogus, I
focused upon the main characters of Dudleytown.

During 1996-1998 I was working on a book about the
William Dudley of Guilford, Connecticut[24] branch of the Dudley
family and the research fit right in for both the genealogical and
Dudleytown projects. In hopes that Cornwall had an historical
society, I picked up the phone (my usual way of obtaining
information fast–God Bless Alexander Graham Bell!) and dialed
the number for information in the area code I believed Cornwall
was in, and Viola! They did!

---

[24]Dudley, Rev Gary P. The New Dudley Genealogies: the
Descendants of William of Guilford 1999, Heritage Books Inc. It was
published in October, 1999.

27

Hurriedly calling the number, I spoke to a Mr. Michael Gannet, then curator of the Cornwall Historical Society. The information he gave was both prophetic and enlightening.

First, Mr. Gannet was very cautious, and I was soon to find out why. Dudleytown, it seems, was a thorn in Cornwall's side. Everyone wanted to know about Dudleytown: its ghosts, history, and where it was–and along came the "ghost hunters," teenagers, and all sorts of undesirable folks into Cornwall, and Dudleytown was being vandalized. I had to assure Mr. Gannet numerous times that I was not a "ghost hunter," but a serious genealogical researcher and a Priest. Once that was established, Mr. Gannet opened up a little, and promised to send me some material. Then came the bomb.

"The society has some folks who have compiled what they call 'group sheets'[25] on many of the residents. Would you like me to send some of them to you? They are based upon town records.[26]"

Would I? You bet!

True to his word, one week later a large manila envelope

---

[25] A Group Sheet is listing of a family, to include parents and children, along with their birth and death dates and places, their parents, and sometimes other information. It is a standard form used by genealogists everywhere to store and share information.

[26] Town Vital Records are the records (usually stored in a town's city hall or court house) listing the birth, marriage, and/or death of a person. If you are lucky, they will also contain the cause of death, and sometimes the parents of the married couple. They are "official" records, and are indispensable to any genealogist. If birth dates are not known, sometimes the Vital Records will contain a baptismal date supplied by the local church. Many Vital Records are now published and are readily available at libraries with genealogical sections, or genealogy societies.

arrived weighing in at a pound and a half. Inside was assorted booklets the society puts out, and the group sheets–which were complete with names, dates, and town vital record numbers. I was in heaven! Here was over a years worth of genealogical work plopped into my mail box! Arming myself with this wonderful storehouse of information, and what I had already discovered, I quickly organized the full picture. We will look at the brothers themselves in the next chapter. Here, for the first time, is the *true* pedigree of the Dudleytown brothers....

William Dudley was born in Richmond, Surrey, England on September 11, 1608.[27] He married Jane Lutman on May 1, 1674. His son William was born aboard the ship "St. John" bound for America on June 8, 1639. His other children are: Joseph, born April 23, 1642; Ruth, born April 20, 1645; and Deborah, born September 20, 1647. The last three children were born in Guilford,

Connecticut.[28]

Son William married Mary Roe on November 4, 1661 in Saybrook. HIS son Joseph was born in Saybrook, Connecticut, on September 14, 1674[29]. There were 10 other siblings, which space prevents me from mentioning.

Joseph married Sarah Pratt on December 10, 1696 in

---

[27]Dean Dudley, pg 341, and any book on Connecticut History can verify this.

[28]All birth information from Guilford Vital Records.

[29]Dean Dudley.

Saybrook, and the couple had 12 children, all born there.[30] They are: (Dudleytown brothers are in **bold**) Sarah (born March 1699), Deborah (November 1701), Israel (March 1704), **Gideon** (1706), Abigail (1708), **Abiel** (baptized May 11, 1710), Joseph (1712), Cyrian (1715), Mehetabel (1718). Jemina (1720), Ester (1723), and **Barzillai**, (baptized April 7, 1725).[31]

So we see that *three* of them *were* brothers.

Now lets us take an in-depth look at the Dudleytown brothers, as THEY are the souls at whose door the entire Legend revolves around.

---

[30]Ibid, pg 348. The Cornwall Vital Records confirmed the birth dates of the Dudleytown brothers.

[31]All birth and Baptism information is from town records. When birth information is not available, baptism dates are sometimes supplied from the local church. Baptism *usually* took place within one month of the birth.

# The Dudleytown Brothers

*"Some wanted to call it Owlsbury, but by shear number the Dudley's won out."*[32]

The Dudleytown brothers are central to our investigation, for it is they that supposedly brought the "curse" into the area, and began the Legend. Reason dictates that if they were cursed, it should be very apparent. Unnatural deaths, or other strange, unusual things *should* have happened to them. The genealogical data I found was *very* contrary to this, as we will see.

As stated, the three Dudleytown brothers were Gideon (who was the first to arrive at Dudleytown), Abiel, and Barzillai. Most of the stories state that the brothers were returning from the French and Indian war. That lasted from 1754-1763.[33] Now we have a HUGE problem. How could these brothers have been returning from something that had not yet happened? Apparently the Legend tellers assume that no one remembers American History—and I am sad to say that most don't. Even some of the pamphlets I have seen denouncing the "Legend (or Curse) of Dudleytown" never point that out–and most even support the brothers as having returned from the French and Indian wars.[34] But let's disregard that for a time, they arrived in the area, and appear on the tax records for Cornwall (Gideon in 1748, Barzillai in 1750, and Abiel in 1754).[35]

---

[32]From many of the "Curse" stories.

[33]See any High School History book

[34]One prime example is Paul H. Chamberlain's Dudleytown, published by the Cornwall Historical Society. Mr. Chamberlain was a former curator of the Society who supplied me the group sheets on the brothers.

[35]Cornwall Tax Records from the stated years.

Now, some stories name an "Abijah" (or some spelling like that). I have never found an Abijah Dudley in the genealogical records. That is because there isn't any. What REALLY happened was that a town scribe in Cornwall simply misspelled the name. During the granting of rights for the property, it is written: "....grantor Abijah Dudly..........said Abiel...." So it was a spelling error, and nothing more. It its truly amazing what actually *reading* the source will do!

The brothers were all from Saybrook (just north of Guilford) Connecticut, a place also noted for a large amount of Dudley's. In fact, Guilford had its own section of its city that was known as "Dudleytown"! Today, about 1/4 of the Dudley's in the U.S. can trace their lineage to the Guilford area.

Gideon bought his land June 24, 1747[36] and was there (in Cornwall) July 7, 1748.[37] He is on the tax records from 1748 to1771, and was last recorded in Cornwall January 13, 1773.[38] He seems to have left after that.

While there, Gideon and wife Elisabeth (sic) added to the family (already consisting of Anna, who was born in 1745, and Louisa, born in 1747). On January 2, 1749, the couple gave birth to Gideon.[39] On February 15, 1752, to daughter Elisabeth was born,

---

[36] Cornwall Land Records Vol.1, page 61. Land Records record the buying and selling of land in the town, and in many areas are LEGAL documents.

[37] Ibid, Vol.1, page 245.

[38] Cornwall Land Records Vol.3, page 310.

[39] All birth and death dates are from Cornwall Vital Records.

and Abigail on May 10, 1754. Last to be born in Dudleytown was a son, Joseph, who was born November 14, 1755. Not all of the children lived, however. Death took many children in those days, and Louisa died when she was 20, on Jan 5, 1767. Little Gideon was just two when he died October 15, 1766, and Joseph was 11 on November 20, 1766 when he also died. Mother Elisabeth also left this earth May 21, 1765. There was nothing untoward in these deaths, however, all were from natural causes. They did not even make the Legend.

A good citizen, Gideon was voted in as Surveyor of Highways and Grand Juryman for the year 1752 at the Cornwall Town meeting held December 9, 1751.[40] Gideon left Dudleytown sometime after January 1773. To where, we have no idea--no record exists of him after that time. He would have been 67 years old then, an old man. Please note that even in the curse, nothing out of the ordinary happened to him. His daughter Anna had married Martin Dudley (NOT a member of the family), and they moved on before Gideon left.

The second brother, Barzillai, bought his land about December 31, 1748,[41] and was in Cornwall by March 6, 1750 when he married Sarah Carter.[42] He was on the tax records for the town from 1750 to 1758. While there, the family had two children, Sibe born May 16, 1750, and Sarah, born February 1, 1752. By looking at the dates, it would seem that Barzillai HAD to have been in Cornwall sooner than his marriage, as Sarah was already pregnant! Be that as it may, nobody in *this* family died. In contradiction to the

---

[40]Cornwall Land Records Vol. 1, page 318.

[41]Cornwall Land Records Vol.1, page 246

[42]Cornwall Vital Records Vol.1, page 13

Legend, *this* Dudleytown brother actually *did* serve in the French and Indian War, for according to the records of those residents of Connecticut involved in the War, there was a "Barzilla Dudley" from Cornwall in Capt. Lyman's Company in 1757 for 14 days.[43] The group of men Barzillai served with responded to the alarm to relieve Fort William Henry. Remembering that Dudleytown is NOT really a town, but part of Cornwall, I believe that it is obvious that this is our Barzillai. If my math is correct, when Barzillai and Sarah left Dudleytown, Barzillai would have been 33. While in Cornwall, he served as Collector "for all town rates for the year ensuing (1751) and the minister's rate for ye year past (1750)."[44]

There is *another* Barzillai Dudley on the records of Haddem, Connecticut, that some say is our Dudleytown Barzillai. I, however, do not think so. For him to have been the same, our Dudleytown Barzillai would have to be fathering children in his 50's. Additionally, the new Barzillai is married to a different woman. I believe this was our Dudleytown Barzillai's son. Whether it is the Dudleytown Barzillai or not, however, has nothing to do with the Dudleytown legend/curse. Nothing strange is recorded for either of them.

This brings us to Abiel. He bought his land on July 7, 1748,[45] when he was in Saybrook, Connecticut. He sold his land to

---

[43]Rolls of Connecticut Men in the French and Indian War, Volume 1, 1903, The Connecticut Historical Society, 1993 Heritage Press Reprint, page 247.

[44]Cornwall Land Records Vol. 1, page 316. Note that Cornwall, like many other New England Towns at that time, paid its local minister by collection *of the town*, NOT the church, as is done today.

[45]Cornwall Land Records Vol.1, page 245

Barzillai on Dec 5, 1748,[46] and apparently moved to Sheffield, Massachusetts where he bought more Cornwall land on October 23, 1753.[47] He shows on the Cornwall Tax Records for the years 1754-1757. On the 16th of December 1771, "Heman Swift of Cornwall ....by virtue of the power and authority given me by the General Assembly" sold Abiel's land to defray town expenditures and became a charge of the town.[48]

Now, Abiel is *always* called the first unusual death there--in fact, the first instance of the "curse." He died a pauper, and was said to be mad. Folks--the man was 90 years old when he died. *NINETY.* Even by today's standards, that is a long life. Back then, it was almost *unheard* of! Remember that in 1799 (the year that he died) there was no Social Security, no medicare; nothing. The children took care of their parents. Unfortunately for "Old Biel", he had none. So who took care of him? NO ONE.[49] When he could no longer afford to pay his debts, the town took his property and sold it, and then put him as a CHARGE of the town. (by the way, it was General Heman Swift that was placed in charge of disposing of his estate--not Barzillai as some have stated) All standard operating procedure at that time. Nothing at all unusual. As a charge, poor Abiel was sent from "foster" house to "foster" house--whomever would take him for the low stipend the town would give to the care giver. A few examples of this come from the Cornwall Town meeting notes: Caleb Jones took Abiel in 1773/4 for "2s7" (two shillings, 7 pence); and Salmon Emons kept him in 1776 for 6

---

[46]Cornwall Land Records Vol.1, page 285

[47]Cornwall Land Records Vol. 2, page 24

[48]Cornwall Land Records Vol.3, page 306

[49]Gideon had left after 1771, and Barzillai after 1758.

pounds to "keep his clothes in good repair, etc."[50]

But didn't he go mad? Well, at a time when the average life expectancy was 40-50 years, what would senility look like? Read the case again, it certainly appears to be senility. He was forgetful, couldn't handle his debts.....think about it.

As stated, a Martin Dudley appears on one of the tax records. Not only that, but he married Gideon's daughter Anna on 21 June 1763.[51] He was from Springfield, Massachusetts,[52] far away from Saybrook (Guilford) Connecticut where the Brothers were from. The solution is simple--he was of a different branch of the Dudley family.

There is a Martin who was involved with the founding of Canandaigua, New York, in 1788-89. This date would be consistent with Martin leaving Dudleytown. As Martin and Anna were newlyweds, it would not be surprising that they would want to begin their new lives in a newly founded town. While there is no hard evidence at the current time to support that it was the SAME Martin, I believe that it very well could be. No matter though, again there is no connection to our curse. He supposedly ran a Tavern, and was referred to as "Captain." The only other Martin Dudley in Connecticut that I am aware of--who belonged to the Dudleytown line--was not born until 1779 to Zebulon Dudley.

Lastly, what of this "LaFayette Dudley"? Yes, there WAS

---

[50]Cornwall Town Meeting notes Vol. 1, pages 9 and 73, respectively.

[51]Cornwall Vital Records of the 1st Congregational Church, page 123.

[52]Cornwall Land Records, Vol 2, page 246

one. He was the minister of the Methodist Church in Cornwall in 1870, about 71 years *after* the last of the original Dudleytown brothers died.[53] He was the proprietor of the later named Housatonic Institute (a school). Was he related? No, he was from the Governor Thomas Dudley branch of the Dudley family, and sent to Cornwall as the minister. The school did not go very well, and he mortgaged the property to M. Beers and Sons. He then tried to use it as a boarding house, but later gave it up. (the Beers did the same thing in reverse order, and they succeeded) He bought a Cemetery plot at the Cornwall Cemetery on what is now Route 4 on February 3, 1879, from Cyrus W. Marsh. LaFayette then went west and died in 1913. He and his wife Sarah Wells Dudley, along with their son William, are buried in the plot they bought in Cornwall.[54] I wonder if he knew of his infamous namesakes?

So now we have a problem. There are NO "cursed" links to any one that had been beheaded, or had any unfortunate thing happen to any of the Dudleytown Dudley's except Abiel's senility. I was becoming very discouraged. Not only was my hope for a "haunted town" being dashed, but the research was just too easy to do. All the while I was beginning to find help in unusual places. I met a person on the internet, one Nancy Ziegler, who was herself writing a book on Dudleytown. She was a member of a Paranormal group called the Cosmic Society, and while her view of Dudleytown was much different from my own, we immediately struck up a friendship that continues to this day. Not all of those people are "weird-o's" some, like Nancy, wanted to know the truth. We immediately started exchanging information. We still do.

---

[53]The Methodist Church in Cornwall disbanded during the 1930's, according to the Cornwall Historical Society.

[54]From Cemetery Records. Remarkably, the Cornwall Vital Records do not reflect either his or his wife's death. This occasionally happens.

On face value, this should end this book. History, genealogy, and common sense has proved—repeat, *proved*–that there was never a link between *anyone* associated with the Dudleytown brothers in the legends of the stories, and *nothing* ever happened that was unusual to any of the three pivotal characters in the story.

And yet there will be some that will *insist* that the FACTS are wrong—but they have to if they are going to arrive at their illogical destination.

During all this time more and more history was coming in about the area and people. Social and area history plays a huge part in the overall picture of any historical event. One prime example is Salem, Massachusetts. At face value, you would think that some kids just went bonkers and started accusing folks of being witches. A closer look at the land and people, however, lend great insights as to why that unfortunate piece of history occurred.

So lets move on to the history and geography of the area. Maybe the land was cursed.

# A Short History of Dudleytown

*"The Almighty from his boundless store*
*Piled rocks on rocks and did no more"*[55]

Because Dudleytown is actually a part of anther town, there has never been a history written about it. Rev. Starr's <u>History of Cornwall</u> does have a short article in it about the history of Dudleytown, but no real written history exists. Therefore, we have to rely on what little Rev. Starr gave us, and check what the "Legend" says concerning it, and then fill in from church and town records. There has been one booklet published by the Cornwall Historical Society that also sheds light on our study. Combining all known sources, here is what can be determined.

Dudleytown was founded in the 1740's (most say 1747) by Thomas Griffis (some town records spell it "Griffin"), who obtained half ownership of the land now known as Dudleytown with George Halloway. The land was acquired at the land auctions in Cornwall that occurred between 1735-95. This had nothing to do with the land grant from Yale University as some have stated. Thomas's land was again sold at auction on June 8, 1796 by Cornwall's tax collector.[56] However, the Property Records show the land being bought on December 7, 1739, when Thomas was in Litchfield.[57] He is recorded as being in Cornwall by April 4,

---

[55]From the diary of Ezra Stiles, describing the area of Dudleytown.

[56]Cornwall Land Records, Vol 7, page 87

[57]Cornwall Property Rights Vol. 2, page 85

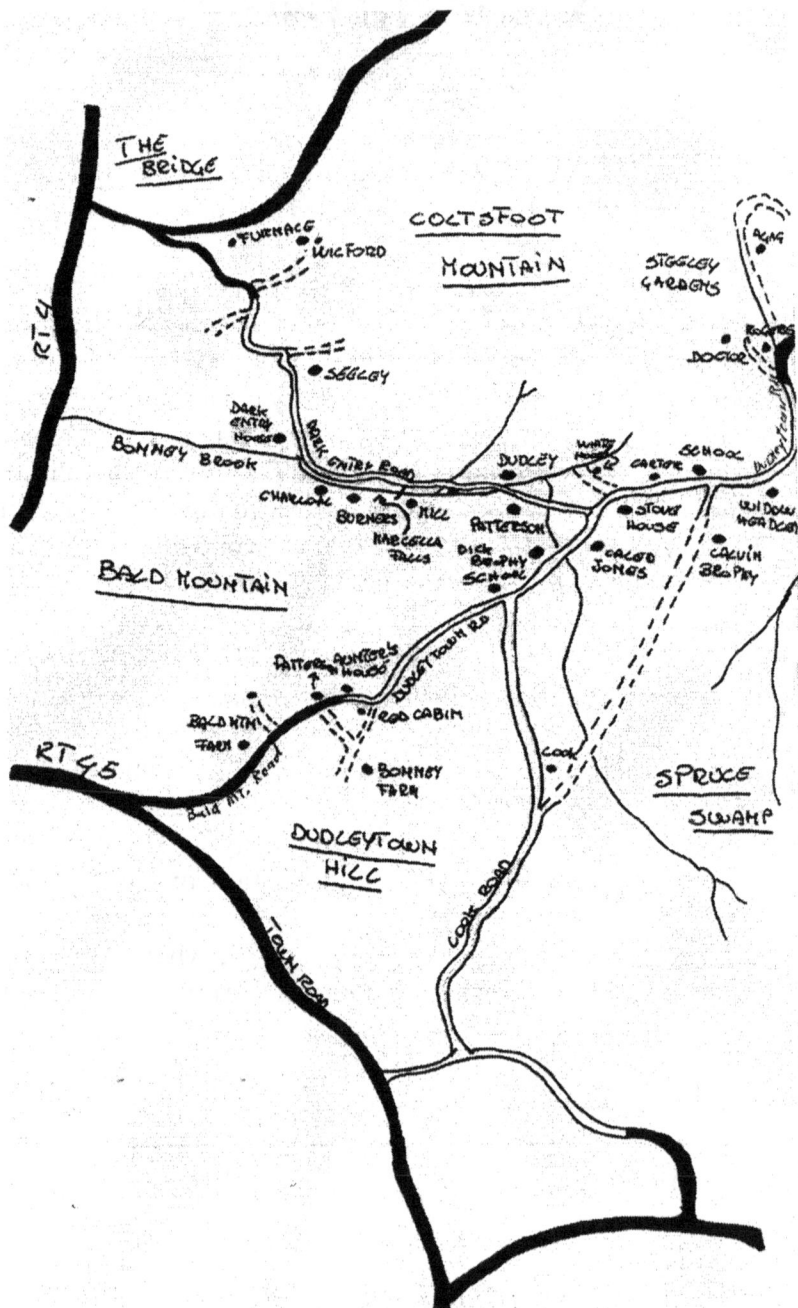

THE BRIDGE

COLTSFOOT MOUNTAIN

RT 4

FURNACE
MACFORD
SEELEY
DARK ENTRY HOUSE
DARK ENTRY ROAD
BONNEY BROOK

DUDLEY
WHITE HOUSE
CARTER
SCHOOL

STEELEY GARDENS
KING
ROGERS
DOCTOR

BALD MOUNTAIN

CHARCOAL
BURROWS
HILL
PATTERSON
MARCELLA FALLS
DICK BROPHY SCHOOL
STOUT HOUSE
CALEB JONES
WIDOW MCDOOM
CALVIN BROPHY

PATTERSON'S HOUSE
HUNTER'S HOUSE
DUDLEYTOWN RD
LOG CABIN
BALD MTN FARM
Bald Mt. Road
BONNEY FARM

COOK
SPRUCE SWAMP

RT 45

DUDLEYTOWN HILL

COOK ROAD

TOWN ROAD

1741,[58] but was undoubtably there earlier. Wether or not Thomas Griffis every really lived in Dudleytown is debated, and he is hardly ever  mentioned in the legend. Most local historians say Thomas settled not far from the border of what was then Kent, now known as Warren.  Thomas died in 1758.[59] The reason most historians point to 1747 is probably because that is the year the first *Dudley* (Gideon) bought land there.

One part of the Dudleytown legend seems to be true. All accounts state that the inhabitants of the area were at first divided about what to call the town. "Owlsbury" *was* in the running, mainly due to the vast number of Horned Owls in the vicinity. Dudleytown won out due to the number of Dudleys in the settlement.

Dudleytown was never a real town. It was, and still is, a part of Cornwall, Connecticut.[60] Cornwall itself had some historical residents, of whom perhaps the most famous being Ethan Allen, whose father was elected a town "selectman" in 1740. Ethan spent a number of years in Cornwall before moving on, most sources saying he went to school there, and was in Cornwall when Dudleytown was at its peak. There are other famous people that some have said came from Dudleytown, but didn't. Samuel Jones has been said to have been mayor of Dudleytown–he wasn't, of course, he was mayor of Cornwall (he was, however, related to the Dudleytown Jones', and as we will see in a later chapter, his

---

[58]Cornwall Land Records Vol 1, page 19

[59]Vital records of 1st Congregational Church pg 32.

[60]There was also a Dibbletown and a Deantown in Cornwall, neither of which are said to be haunted.

grandson is granted a place in history). Throughout the remainder of this book, and *any* book or article containing a Dudleytown story, it is *very* important to remember that Dudleytown was *never* a town of its own, but a part of Cornwall.

Cornwall was a typically Colonial township, so when reading about life in Colonial America, all the little nuances can be applied to it. Cornwall was very aware of all the news in the

Visitors to Dudleytown view a cellar hole–all that remains of the town.

Colonies, and many of it's residents took part in the history of the times (i.e. the French and Indian War, and the Revolution). In fact, at a town meeting on August 22, 1774, it took special notice of the "Boston Port Bill" which closed the Port of Boston. The closing of the Port, was part of the "Intolerable Acts" that were inflicted on the Colonies due to the Boston Tea Party. The town supported the Colonists actions (in regard to the Tea Party), and supported them.[61]

---

[61]Cornwall Town Meeting notes Vol. 1, page 76.

## The Legend of Dudleytown

The actual location of Dudleytown has caused a little confusion. Some maps seem to indicate that it is actually on what is now named Dudleytown Hill. Other maps almost make it appear that it sits in a valley between several hills, or on Bald Mountain itself. Descriptions cause further confusion. To end this, careful research shows that Dudleytown sits on a plateau in the middle of hills: Bald Mountain; Dudleytown Hill; and Woodbury Mountain. The location accounts for the near darkness even at noon. (it also accounts for the constant hooting of the owls!) It was never actually on a hill of its own. Dudleytown Hill got its name after the settlement began.

To try to get any sort of picture as to what the plateau and area around Dudleytown was like, you really must look at Cornwall and observe the trees there. Most historians would agree that the flora and fauna of Cornwall would be an accurate representation of what Dudleytown was at one time. Large white pines, giant hemlocks, and the native chestnut trees abound. Cornwall itself is somewhat famous for its Cathedral Pines. Add to that the rocky ground, and then imagine the Dudley brothers in the middle of all this with nothing more than an axe. In order to get anything done, the trees had to be chopped down--even to just build a fence. The ground was not suited to planting anything, and while small vegetable gardens (such as potatoes, onions, and turnips) did survive, Dudleytown was never renowned for any of its crops. Everything needed for everyday life had to be bought in from Cornwall on the main roads.

There were no stores, and no meeting houses. There wasn't even a church in Dudleytown--the spiritual needs were met in the Congregational Church in Cornwall Plain, and the neighboring town of Warren. When a resident died, a trip to Cornwall was necessary as there wasn't even a graveyard in Dudleytown.

There were a few schools, the closest being District School #10 located at the northern foot of Agag Mountain (the Dudleytown area itself was in District #13, which was technically serviced by Bald Mountain school). There was another school on the southern foot of Agag, whose longest resident school teacher was a man named Sam Dean. There is one other school shown on the map, locate right below Dick Brophy's house at the intersection of Dudleytown and Cook roads. (see map) No one I talked to–the Historical Society, DEF members, and others, knew anything about the school. It appears on the map, and no where else. It could be that it was a school that was planned for that location, and never built. As for people, the population of the Dudleytown area never exceeded 100--if it ever got close to that number. Considering that there are approximately 10 cellar holes (or "root" cellars, as some call them) left, and allowing for the same number of above ground dwellings that didn't have cellars, this seems about right. According to a 1854 map of Cornwall, (a modified version appears on a previous page) there were 26 families located in Dudleytown, and this is assumed to have been the most at any time.[62] In fact, the entire population of Cornwall hardly exceeded 1,400 at its peak, and still hasn't broken 2,000. Some local historians put the population of Dudleytown far below 100, a few as low as 50, most of the time of its existence.

As with all Colonial towns, most of the people lived on the two main roads that ran through Dudleytown: Dark Entry Road, where Gideon Dudley and the Patterson's lived; and Dudleytown Road, where the Carter's (who owned Abiel Dudley's home), and the Jones' had their houses. Cook Road was, of course, named after the Cook family.

---

[62]"Dudleytown, Cornwall's Deserted Village", by Brainerd T. Peck, in <u>My Country</u> Magazine, Vol. 22, No.2, Summer 1988, page 7.

## The Legend of Dudleytown

So why is Dudleytown believed to have been a "full-blown" town with churches, graveyards, stores, etc? No one knows. Apparently the original Dudleytown story tellers never bothered to do any research on it.

It would seem odd to the casual visitor why a town would fail in the Cornwall area. There is so much fertile soil......until you get to the Dudleytown location. As Dudleytown is in the hills, it and had its soil washed away by (geologists claim) glaciers and water running downhill. Remember, Dudleytown is at an elevation of 1,500 feet, over 1,000 feet higher than Cornwall Plain. In addition to all of the above, there are what some present day residents call "fairy caves," which are gaps in the stones which have been covered over by grass. One wrong move and your foot is stuck fast. If you are able to remove it, a sprained ankle or broken foot could be the result. These are all over the area, and undoubtably are to blame for so many missing cattle and other livestock that belonged to the early residents. Once stuck, they were an easy meal for the wildlife of the area.

Wildlife flourishes in the area. Bobcats, snakes, white tailed deer, a few black bear, and chipmunks abound there. Several species of birds inhabit the area, including grouse, woodpeckers, and the famous owls. Residents will readily talk about the wildlife–but many visitors never see any. In fact, most remark that there is *no* wildlife there, and it is dead (pardon the pun) silent in Dudleytown. A possible explanation for this is that wildlife does not like humans, and will usually leave the area. In addition, should a predator wonder into the area, an unhuman silence will occur quickly. Hunters will quickly relate to this. Remarkably, most of the reports of silence in the area that I have received came from those unfamiliar with forest life. There seem to have been rattlesnakes in the area in the beginnings of the Cornwall/Dudleytown era, as some of the town meeting notes refer to them. In my visit to Dudleytown in 1999, I saw a lot of wildlife, most noticeably chipmunks and birds.

Of the small crops that Dudleytown did produce, perhaps the most revealing is rye---used to make bread. If one is experienced in making bread, you are well aware that if rye is left for any length of time, it goes bad. The resulting mold is almost a hallucinogen......yes, it makes you see things, and it could also kill you. Could that account for the supposed sightings of demons? If not, it is at least something to think about! That is, if you *must* believe that anyone actually saw any demons. There are no records—absolutely zero—of anyone seeing anything throughout the history of Dudleytown. Also, the town did grow flax--but barely enough for the local people to sustain themselves.

Dudleytown was noted for its timber, usually burnt and used to make wood coal for the nearby Litchfield County Iron Furnaces, in Cornwall and other towns, and for making charcoal. Local pictures taken in the 1800's show Cornwall as almost depleted of its trees.[63] Many books state that Dudleytown was in the same situation. When the Furnaces moved closer to the railway, and more industrial towns, then there was no need for all that timber. Add to that the invention of the Bessimer process in the late 1800's, and the very reason for Dudleytown's existence, along with that of Cornwall, begins to disappear. While we are on the subject, let us remember that all those trees being felled provided little to stop rains from washing away what topsoil there was! Pictures of Cornwall from the Dudleytown times shows only a few apple trees left.

Charcoal was used for many things during early Colonial

---

[63]Unfortunately, few of these pictures survive, and are extremely hard to obtain.

times: cleaning your teeth, purifying water, settling upset stomachs, storing ice, and freshening ones breath. Making charcoal required Charcoal Burning people, which the town called "Raggies." They were called Raggies, not because of their appearance (as terrible as the residents thought it was), but because the earliest of them came from Mount Riga (according to some local historians). Their job required them to stand beside the charcoal burners all day, and most had the appearance of being black, despite the fact that many were European (or, as some say, Middle Eastern). Many Raggies were new immigrants, and spoke little English. As charcoal became easier to make, most of the Raggies moved on, and those that remained gained an unsavory reputation, with many folk saying they all were "crazy." You can still find some remnants of the charcoal mounds in the Dudleytown area.

There is Iron Ore in this area—much in Dudleytown, and even more in nearby Salisbury. That, along with all the trees, could very well explain the lightning strikes in Dudleytown and the surrounding area (which would explain the death of General Swift's wife). One person told me that there are more lightning strikes in that area than anywhere else they knew. Yet, they went on to say that Cornwall had the most (again, not realizing that Dudleytown is part of Cornwall). I would imagine that they have never been to the plains States. At any rate, so much Iron Ore and trees would make anything vulnerable to strikes. Additionally, glacial rock and granite are abundant.

There were three water powered mills in Dudleytown, one ground limestone for plaster in making houses; another a grist mill. It is unknown what the third was, but is supposed by some to have been a saw mill.[64] The main water supply, used to power at least

---

[64]Clark, Harriet Lydia, <u>True Facts About Dudleytown</u>, 1989, Cornwall Historical Society, page 7.

one of these mills, and also supplied the drinking water for Dudleytown, came from Bonney Brook, which still exists there and marks the border for Dark Entry Forest Inc.'s land holdings on Dark Entry Road. The mills closed when they were no longer needed due to the loss of the timber trade, and because of the long trip down the mountain to deliver their goods. There were farms also, mostly near the bottom of the hill.

The land used to belong to Mohawk Indians, some say. History shows that while there were Indians in the area, the only major Indian trail ran through northern Cornwall, not the Dudleytown area. There are one or two versions of the Legend, and some local native Americans and Paranormal groups, that say Dudleytown was built on top of an Indian Burial Ground. Of note, *these* versions and stories did not start until (amazingly) after the movie "Poltergeist" came out.[65] History shows that the nearest Indian burial ground was about 30 miles away. In 1955, there was a flood, and the authorities decided to build what is now Sucker Brook Dam right on top of the burial ground.

Dudleytown, like other towns in the Colonial times, was visited by disease. Two epidemics ran through the town (and throughout all of Cornwall)--one in August 1774, and the other in 1813. Scores of people died during them. What is surprising, though, is that some writers actually have laid these epidemics on the *curse*. These Legend tellers insist that they were "epidemics of unknown origin," but most historians say that Cornwall was fortunate to have only have had two of them. Remember that sanitary conditions were bleak at best until after the Civil War, and during this era simple childhood diseases such as measles, mumps,

---

[65]The movie "Poltergeist" is based on a haunting that occurs in a house built on top of a Native American burial ground, and is the reason for the haunt.

cholera, chicken pox, and small pox, were all common "epidemics" in the early years of our country, and many died from them.

After DEF bought the land, there seems to have been fields of various berries, as most of the residents speak of going into them and picking various types, most notably blackberries and blueberries. These fields are mostly gone now, but some areas of berries remain, and are still picked.

Cornwall Cemetery

The Appalachian Trail ran through Dudleytown for more than 65 years. The 1966 National Scenic Trails Act provided that the Appalachian Trail, and a few other designated trails across the nation, were all to be on public lands or have permanent easements. In response to that, perhaps two thirds of the Appalachian Trail in Connecticut has been relocated. The largest part of this move was about 1980. Earlier the trail ran to the east across the bridge at Cornwall Bridge, then up Dark Entry and looped east, then north, then west and back across the Housatonic at Falls Village. The Appalachian Trail is now entirely west of the Housatonic (except for a short stretch at Falls Village), largely on existing Connecticut State Forest lands. Part of what was The Appalachian Trail near Dudleytown was renamed the Mohawk Trail, and is being maintained.

So why did all the people leave Dudleytown/Cornwall? Considering the decline of the town, you have to ask what was there to keep the young, and the newly married in Dudleytown, or Cornwall for that matter? There were no factories, as all were victims of the Bessimer Process. There were no large farms, especially in Dudleytown, and no textiles. No economic means to support the settlement at all. As the iron factories diminished, so did many jobs. So, with the Westward Expansion in full force, the young moved on to better opportunities, jobs in other towns or other states, and once established never returned to Dudleytown/Cornwall. In fact, Mrs. Clark comments that letters she has found by those who left Dudleytown *encouraged* the remaining residents to join *them*![66]

Let us remember, however, that Dudleytown did survive over 100 years. It was long-lived for Colonial towns of the time. It was, perhaps, one of the first of the New England areas that simply died due to its location.

Before we go on though---when, exactly, did Dudleytown die? Well, that, of course, depends on whom you read. We will cover that in full in a later chapter, but for now suffice it to say that the "curse" tellers would have it dead after Dr. Clark. This is, in fact, both true and false. As a viable town, sources say that there wasn't a permanent resident left after the chestnut blight of 1900. That is true--but people did (and still do, by the way) build some houses in the "recognized" Dudleytown area after that time. Some residents in the area still pick berries there, and there still are one or two occupied houses (near the bottom of the hill). According to most Cornwall historians, however, the death of Dudleytown began

---

[66]Clark, pages 6 and 7.

with the depletion of the trees, and invention of the Bessimer Process–shortly thereafter the mills shut down, and the town, as a viable living part of Cornwall, was abandoned by 1900. At least at the top of the hill.

So what is Dudleytown today? Some say it was so cursed that the state removed it from maps in the 1970's to keep people away from it! While we will look at the situation in depth in the chapter on DEF, let us just touch on it by saying that the truth is that the area (all 850 acres of it) is owned by Dark Entry Forest, Inc. (DEF). They are maintaining it as a wildlife refuge–when people are not vandalizing it.

With the information I had found, I really started to wonder about how anyone could have believed this legend. The answer is....the deaths! I had already solved the death of Abiel, and it was time to look at the others. *Could* these deaths be explained? It should be easy for a genealogist–just obtain the town vital records and hope a cause of death is listed. If I couldn't find those, perhaps some local history books would have the answers. I found both. Not only were many of the town records sent to me by the Cornwall Historical Society, but there are TWO Histories of Cornwall written–the most obtainable being Rev. Starr's *History of Cornwall*.[67] Most of the deaths were covered in Star's History, the rest were in the records, and I gobbled up the information as quickly as I could read it.

I was totally surprised at the answers I found in the Histories of the town and the Vital Records. Surprised not only by the simplicity of finding the town histories (one was right in my local library), but also surprised by the commonness of the deaths.

---

[67]The other is Gold's History, and is difficult to find.

And I was shocked by how much the Legend tellers changed the facts to fit their story.

# The Deaths at Dudleytown

"What is truth?"-Pontius Pilate

According to the legend, the strange deaths at Dudleytown are the very backbone of our story. Already noting that there is absolutely no basis for a curse through the town's namesakes, the deaths are also the *only* proof left that anything mysterious even happened. Lets examine the deaths and unusual happenings at Dudleytown one by one in the light of town records and printed history. Unlike many of our "curse" stories, these are presented here chronologically as to the date of the occurrence–not the date of the 'legend tellers' or even the date that I found the solution. Note that some of the backgrounds of these deaths were to be found in Rev. Starr's *History of Cornwall*, available at any large library. I will plainly state where any additional information came from.

1737-1799-THE ORIGINAL DUDLEY'S. All of the information concerning the Dudleytown brothers are in a former chapter. I will only remind you that all of them seemed to have died of natural causes. Should a "curse" had been placed upon the brothers, or had they been heirs to one, they *should* have died unusual deaths. However, all the deaths were ordinary.

1763--THE CARTER FAMILIES . Nathaniel Carter supposedly set the "curse" in motion by buying Abiel Dudley's house when "Old Biel" became a charge of the town. They lived in Dudleytown for four years until they decided to move out in 1763. We have read what happened to them, but was it the "curse?" Let us first remember where they moved--hundreds of miles from Dudleytown. To believe that the "curse" had anything to do with them, we must accept that somehow, someway, this curse attached itself to the Carter's and followed them. But why? What did the Carters have to do with the Dudleys? Should a "curse" on the Dudley name be involved, then why didn't Abiel die mysteriously? Lets move on to the realm of common sense.

The full story of the Carters will be discussed in full in the chapter "A Few Loose Ends" near the end of the book, for now be aware that they moved near Binghamton New York, and built a house at the Forks of the Delaware wilderness. SMACK in the middle of Indian country at the end of the French and Indian War. What did they expect? What happened to the children that were carried away? Well, son David went on to work for the Department of Indian Affairs!

Who bought the Abiel/Carter house afterwards? We are not told. Why? Because nothing happened to the new owners. But the *other* Carters, those that remained in Dudleytown, didn't *they* die strangely? No, they died in the plague of 1774, along with half of Dudleytown and nearby Cornwall.

1792. THE HOLLISTER MURDER. According to most of the stories, Gershon Hollister was murdered at the home of William Tanner. Then, depending on what version of the Legend you read, Tanner started talking about wild animals and demons, and then went totally insane.

There has been a little confusion concerning the *place* of Gershon's death. The confusion arose because some records state that he died at "Widow Hoadley's barn raising, and others at William Tanner's. Again, genealogy comes to the rescue! Gershon Hollister was killed September 23, 1793, at Widow Hoadley's barn raising when he fell from an uncompleted structure,[68] (according to one source, his wife Sarah and son Philemon, only three at the

---

[68]Sedgwick, Charles F. <u>General History of the Town of Sharon</u>, Amenia, N.Y. Charles Walsh, printer. 1877, pg 140.

time, were there). Now, the good Widow was *William Tanner's daughter.* William Tanner was living with her at the time.[69] There is no indication that there was an investigation, as this sort of thing, while unfortunate, was not unheard of. William Tanner was never charged with or convicted of anything. What happened to Tanner? He lived to be 104! That's right, 104. I am not sure, but he could have been the oldest person in the U.S. at that time. He did not go mad–the records indicated "slightly demented" or "feeble minded." Feeble Mindedness *was* a common term used in association with elderly people, and physicians will readily tell you that it meant senility. Again, we *MUST remember the time we are dealing with.* For the first time, we see the "curse tellers" taking history and totally changing it. *None* of the town records, or histories, state anything about a murder. It is never mentioned. Unfortunately, it will not be the last time history will be changed.

1804. GENERAL SWIFT'S WIFE. According to the legend, his wife Sarah Faye was struck by lightning in the head and killed on April 17th, 1804, right on her front porch while the General was out helping George Washington. Afterward, according to the "curse" stories, he went mad!

General Heman Swift *was* an aid to George Washington. The spelling of his first name is correct here. Most of the legend stories add an "r" making it Herman. He was also a resident of Cornwall, and was its Justice of the Peace for some time, arriving there about 1769. As any good citizen would, he took a great interest in the affairs of his community. It was he who was charged with selling Abiel Dudley's property, paying what debts the sale

---

[69]Starr, Rev Edward C. History of Cornwall, 1928, page 473, and Cornwall Vital Records.

would cover, and putting him as a charge of the town.[70] While a Dudleytown resident getting struck by lightning and killed may sound strange, we have a problem. The Good General did not live in Dudleytown. He never did. His house is still on the main Cornwall road, directly across from Bald Mountain Road. (It's a historical landmark, look it up if you are ever there. Careful, though, it's occupied.) As for the General going mad, this didn't happen till he was very old, and the best sources do *not* say mad, but "slightly demented." It seems that the poor men of Dudleytown just can't get old without someone saying they are mad! By the way, the good General outlived *four* wives, of whom Sarah was the third.

So was he home, or off with Washington?

---

[70]Clark, Harriet Lydia <u>True Facts About Dudleytown,</u> 1989, The Cornwall Historical Society.

While he was in Cornwall in 1771 to sell Abiel's home to pay for the debt, he undoubtably left during the Revolution to help in the Continental Army. He returned afterwards, and the tragedy occurred in 1804. Washington DIED in 1799, so he could *not* have been with Washington. Here again, history gets in the way of a legend.

Some "curse" tellers point to the town records for "proof" that this death was a result of something strange. In the town records, you see, there is what *looks* to be a "hand" pointing to the entry of Sarah Faye Swift's death. I have reproduced it here for your consideration. It is an obvious addition—perhaps put there to point out the death of the wife of an historical figure. Nothing more.

Please remember that when reading any historical document, the people writing it do so with the understanding of their *time*. There was no mass media in the early years of our country, and lightning strikes *were* a strange phenomena to them. We now know that they happen every day.

1872. HORACE GREELEY'S WIFE. The legend says that the "curse" of Dudleytown attached itself to Mary Cheney, who was born and raised there, and that she committed suicide!

This bit of information was a little hard to find for a fledgling genealogist—I actually had to think about it, and do some research. She is not listed in the Cornwall vital records, nor was she in the Barbour Collection of Connecticut Vital Records for Cornwall. She was in Starr's *History,* but there were no town records anywhere to back him up. Then I did what any decent historical researcher would do, I headed for the Library.

Figuring that Horace Greeley would have been in the papers

quite a bit due to his bid for the Presidency, and knowing that the Legend stated that his wife committed suicide just before the election, I was pretty sure that her death would probably have made the papers. I had to make an important decision. There were only two places I believed a Presidential Candidate would stay during the last months before the election--New York City or Washington D.C. I opted for New York first, and got very lucky. I looked up a listing for an obituary in the <u>New York Times Index to Obituaries,</u> and Viola! There was one on October 31, 1872, and it contained all that I needed to complete the picture. As any genealogist knows, however, obituaries *can* contain erroneous information, I filled in the rest of her story with information from the Litchfield Historical Society, and biographies of Horace Greeley. With the information obtained from all the sources, here is what I found:

Mary G. Cheney was born October 20, 1811 in Litchfield, Connecticut, to Silas E. and Mary "Polly" Young Cheney,[71] not Cornwall. How did the Legend tellers get this wrong? Easy. Cornwall was in Litchfield COUNTY. A person from there would write that they were from: "Cornwall, Litchfield, Connecticut." Mary was born in the county seat, "Litchfield, Litchfield, Connecticut." Her father was a noted cabinet maker and had two other children–Charlotte Marie and Edward Porter. There are living descendants in the town even today.[72] Mary attended (as did her siblings, and father) the Academy in Litchfield. Upon her graduation in 1829, she left Litchfield and took a job teaching school in Warrentown, North Carolina. There she lived at a vegetarian boarding house owned by Dr. Sylvester Graham–of

---

[71] Litchfield Vital Records vol. 2, pg 12..

[72] In fact, one of them is the *Curator* of the Litchfield Historical Society, whom helped me to confirm this information. They have an entire "Cheney File" about their noted resident.

# OBITUARY

## Mrs. Horace Greeley,

The wife of Mr. Horace Greeley died in this City yesterday morning, at the residence of Mr. Alvin J. Johnson, No. 823 West Fifty-seventh-street. The immediate cause of death was a very severe attack of lung disease, a complaint which had caused her much continued suffering for nearly twenty years. Mrs. Greeley's maiden name was Mary Young Cheney, and she was born at Litchfield, Conn., in the year 1814. Enjoying unusual educational advantages, Miss Cheney became a schoolteacher of rare abilities. Becoming an ardent believer in the hygienic teachings of Dr. Graham, the famous dietist, she frequented the Graham House Hotel, in this City, and there made the acquaintance of her future husband. In the beginning of 1836 she accepted an engagement as teacher in Warrenton, N. C., and married Mr. Greeley at that place in July of the same year.

During her last illness, Mrs. Greeley was attended by Mr. Greeley and her two daughters, the Misses Ida and Gabrielle. From the first it was feared that the attack would have a fatal tendency, and her death was anticipated this week as inevitable, so that her friends were fully resigned to the worst. The funeral will take place in Dr. Chapin's Church on Friday, at the hour of noon, and will be quite private. The body will be conveyed to Green-Wood and buried there in the modest vault which belongs to the family. Her loss will be deeply felt by her family and a large circle of friends.

Mary Cheney Greeley's obituary from the New York Times of October 30, 1870

"Graham Cracker" fame.[73] Apparently, she was involved with the whole "wellness" movement that was catching on throughout the country at the time. Dr. Kellogg, (of "Corn Flakes" fame) had one also, immortalized in the movie *Welcome to Wellville*. While at the boarding house, she met and married Horace "go west young man, go west!" Greeley on July 5, 1836, and followed him like a dutiful wife. During their long marriage, they had seven children.

Please note that there is no indication that she ever set foot in Cornwall. In fact, there is more than ample evidence that she didn't. First of all, Litchfield sits on the other side of hills from Cornwall, and a trip there would have been an all day affair. As Litchfield was the County seat, all the amenities that she would have wanted, and then some, would have been there, and there would have had to have been a specific reason for her to make the journey to Cornwall. Secondly, she seems to have left for Warrentown, North Corolina immediately following her graduation. Next, consider that the Litchfield Historical Society has a large file on the Cheneys, complete with a lot of correspondence between the Cheney family and Greeley. None of the letters even mention Cornwall. Lastly, neither the Cornwall or Litchfield Historical Societies find any documented evidence to indicate that she was ever in the town.[74]

Greeley ran for president against General Ulysses S. Grant in what most would say was an election of forgone conclusion–no one could win against a Civil War hero. His party was the newly formed "Liberal Republicans," and Grant waged one of the most

---

[73]Here is some trivia for you! Dr. Graham was a eccentric Clergyman who invented his famous Cracker in 1829.

[74]This is, of course, overlooking the obvious mistake that one or two Cornwall writers made in saying that Mary *came* from Dudleytown.

vicious campaigns imaginable. Greeley once said during this time: "I don't know if I am running for the Presidency or the Penitentiary!" The stress had to have been terrible, as not only was he fighting a malicious campaign, but his wife Mary was sick.[75]

History records the outcome of the campaign, but just before the election, Mary suffered from a severe attack of lung disease, (which she had for 20 years) and died October 30, 1872. Two of her children, daughters Ida and Gabrielle were in attendance, as her death had been anticipated.[76] She died in New York City and is buried in Green Wood Cemetery. Her husband Horace died one month later on November 29th, and the 40 electoral votes he received were distributed to minor candidates.

While town documents and the obituary point to the fact that Mary was *not* "born and raised" in Dudleytown, I am still left to wonder why so many, including the Cornwall Historical Society and Starr's History of the town, state that she was. Some have postulated that, as a school teacher, Mary *may* have taught school in Dudleytown. This, however, can not be confirmed as most of the school records do not survive. Be that as it may, the facts are clear, Mary Cheney was born in Litchfield, and died in New York of Lung disease.

Here again we face the "curse" totally changing historical facts. If only someone had checked them.

1901. JOHN PATRICK BROPHY. Ah, here is a really strange one. He had supposedly bought the old Colonel Rogers Place (the good Colonel had died naturally). Some of the "curse" stories record

---

[75]Encyclopedia of American Biographies.

[76]New York Times obituary, October 31, 1872, page 6.

him as John Brophy, some as Patrick Brophy. Now, depending on who is telling the story, his children disappeared; his wife died "mysteriously"; his house burns down; and he disappears.

The Brophy family was not new to Dudleytown (see the map–there are two Brophy houses). The first two to arrive was Richard and Calvin Brophy. Richard bought Sam Griffin's house after Sam died. It was on Dudleytown Road just below where Dudleytown Road and Dark Entry meet. It was a pretty little thing with lilacs and a barn in the back. Calvin's house was on Dudleytown above Dark Entry. When Calvin left, John Patrick bought it. The house, then, stayed in the family. All attended the Catholic Church down in Cornwall Bridge. They would appear to have been a very typical family of the period. But what about all the strange things?

Here are the *facts* behind the Brophy incident: his children started stealing "sleigh robes" (those are the blankets you use for warmth on a sleigh ride), and the law was after them. What did they do? They left to escape prison! His wife died of a very common disease of the time, "consumption"–which any doctor will tell you is tuberculosis. The house burned in 1901, and Brophy turned up missing right after that. Or not. The town history plainly records this entire affair, and simply states that Mr. Brophy left.[77]

What would you do? Your sons are running from the law, your wife is dead, and your house just burnt down. Would you sick around and build another house, or leave? You decide.

Dr. WILLIAM COGSWELL CLARKE. Here is an interesting and unfortunate story. What all the legend tellers fail to remember is

---

[77] The incident is recorded in Starr, pg 26.

that this happening is so recent that there are still people living in the area that knew the Doctor!

This was also the hardest of the stories to figure out–and there are still some missing pieces. The problem is that there are still some relatives alive in Cornwall, and with the mystery surrounding his association with a section of town that has caused so much grief for the little town of Cornwall, and due to the first wife's suicide, no one really wanted to talk about him. Understanding and relating to their feelings, I did not press them for information. There were others willing to talk, albeit cautiously. Then an amazing thing happened: one day I returned home from work to find an email letter from Dr. Clarkes' granddaughter! I was totally elated. She asked for my address, and within a week a letter from his actual daughter was in my mail box. The information she passed on was awesome, and she only asked me to keep a few things private (which I most heartily agreed to). Her information, combined with additional research and records, is found below.

Dr. William Cogswell Clarke was born July 2, 1871. He was raised on a farm in Tenafly, New Jersey. He never lived in New York, but commuted there. He was a pathologist and Professor of Surgery, and bought his property, not in 1920 as the storytellers cite, but 1900.[78] What land did he buy? According to his daughter, he bought the actual plateau that the original settlement of Dudleytown was on, and some other acreage there (most people would say that it is on the *opposite* of Bald Mountain Farm, on what is still called Dudleytown road). It is on the additional acreage that he built his first home. He traveled to Dudleytown on some weekends to build his house, and during the summers until its completion. He and his wife Harriet, along with their son William Junior, then visited it during the summer, and

---

[78] Ibid, pg 288.

occasionally on some holidays. The family would later call the home "Crooked House", based, according to Dr. Clarke's daughter, after the nursery rhyme "there was a crooked man, who lived in a crooked house." Then came the unfortunate occurrence.[79] Harriet died in New York City at a hospital. That had to have occurred *before* 1920. Two living relatives say it was either 1917 or 1918, based upon her dying six years after the birth of a son which occurred in 1911. But here's an oddity–while Starr's short biography of the Doctor in his *History* states that he did not return to the house, all other sources, including living relatives, and a later entry in Starr, say he *did* continue to visit the house.[80] While Dr. Clarke did stop spending his summers in the dwelling in Dudleytown,[81] he did not do so until *after* he bought approximately 300 acres on Route 45, and built a brick house there. He began bringing other Doctors and Nurses with him, and on December 9, 1924[82] they incorporated the *Dark Entry Forest, Inc.,* (DEF) which OWNS the Dudleytown area today. At that time, he gave the land he bought, minus some land for his families use, to DEF. The stated purpose of the organization declares that it exists to keep the "naturalness" of the area "in perpetuity." He also married a fine woman named Carita, and on February 1, 1926, DEF had its first meeting with 41 members. William and Carita are listed. They had two children (a number of his grandchildren still reside in the area, and are members of DEF). He died in Cornwall Bridge on

---

[79] It is believed by all the living relatives I spoke to that Harriet never actually had a breakdown of any sort while in the dwelling at Dudleytown. Most believe that it was concocted by the story tellers. Additionally, there is disagreement as to whether Harriet ever really committed suicide.

[80] Ibid.

[81] "Crooked House" was sold during World War Two.

[82] The Charter for the Dark Entry Forest, Inc.

Valentine's day, February 14, 1943.[83] Now think about that for a moment. If his wife went mad from supernatural means, or *any* other way that might tip the good Doctor off that something was amiss, then why did he help to found an organization that would buy the area, then move there himself, and later die there? He was even on the Board of Directors of DEF from 1927–1928.

Dr. Clarke's occurrence at Dudleytown is where most of the "curse" stories end. On face value, it may seem a little odd, to be sure. However, most people familiar to the case will plainly state that they remember that the first wife, Harriet, had an ongoing mental problem.

So there are all the deaths at Dudleytown that are reported by the legend. As you can see, every one of them was recorded by town records when they occurred in Cornwall/Dudleytown, or by history when not.

Let's take stock now as to what we know. First, if you add up all the deaths and divide it by the years the town existed, you will find that there was only one death every seven to ten years. This is not bad, considering the times. This does not, of course, take into account those who died by obvious natural causes. Another way of looking at this is that there was ONE "supernatural" occurrence every 15 years (and that is IF you accept all the deaths as supernatural). Well, if it is a curse, we have to concede that this is not a very active one.

Now let's do something else: let's eliminate the natural deaths, and the ones we now know were changed. You then have Sarah Swift, and......no one. One death that was odd in 165 years. One.

---

[83]From his Cremation Permit.

We can now see that nothing out of the ordinary ever happened in Dudleytown. History has *again* disproved the Legend of Dudleytown. Now there only remain the modern "happenings."

# The other Paranormal Happenings

I had originally planned a long psychological explanation for the newer "events," but a very enlightening coincidence occurred in the summer of 1997 that helped quite a bit. I received an email from a person named Brian Maurisello, who worked with Jeff Ballenger, and the two of them were attempting to film a documentary on Dudleytown. Brian came to my house that summer and filmed an interview with me. I only spoke with Jeff over the phone. While the documentary project was not successful, the conversations with Jeff were quite productive. He reveled quite a bit from his associations with other writers, film makers, and a few key characters associated with Dudleytown. The following information was gleaned from this interview.

**THE TV STATION CREW.** This one is reported by our old friends Ed and Lorraine Warren. The crew went up to film a story and their equipment would not work. You can read about it in Ghost Hunters. Here are the facts: the crew worked for a local COMCAST cable access station. It is a small station, with a small, underpaid crew that is equipped with cameras and things that the other stations no longer used. The fact is, they *did* get footage at Dudleytown--before their equipment broke! When they got back, they joked: "It's the curse of Dudleytown again!" However, some people took it seriously. Most of the crew still live and work in the area. In fact, there have even been other film crews there. There was one from SUNY (State University of New York) Purchase in 1992. I videotaped my own visit to Dudleytown in1999. No problems occurred with my taping.

**OTHER SIGHTINGS**. According to various "Ghost Hunters" and other paranormal folks who have been there, Dudleytown has vortexes,[84] UFO sightings, ball lightning, "globulars," bigfoots, etc. Can you see how one or two strange instances in a town, no longer in existence, can turn into a legend? At first, just stories about ghosts and "hoofed" creatures and now the entire paranormal menagerie. Again, during the time this town existed, *not one* instance of a ghost or demon was reported. Letters exist by folks that lived there, town records, tax records, and the local Church record are there to be checked. Nothing.

*Remember the time period.* If these folk actually thought they were "haunted" or besieged by the devil, they *would* have let someone know, and ministers from everywhere would have descended upon the town to "do battle with the devil." They didn't.

So what about the *hundreds* of sightings reported on the Internet and in books? All we have there is personal experience. How reliable is that? I would be tempted to say that it depends on the person reporting it. Consider, for instance, the experiments reported by crime classes in various universities throughout the nation. You may have seen some on TV. A class is in session, someone comes into the room and either steals, does, or says something, then leaves. The class is told to write what they saw/heard. Everyone reports something different. Now consider the following quote from Dody Clarke, a resident of Cornwall Bridge, and the current president of Dark Entry Forest, Inc.:

---

[84]A "vortex" (depending on whom you speak to) is an "energy center." "Globulars" are "balls of energy" usually (according to "experts") representing ghosts. I received one email claiming that the person had seen a "bigfoot," and one person actually told me about one. Actually, the "entire paranormal menagerie" I speak of is *not* an exaggeration. People have reportedly been "slapped," pushed, seen ghosts, heard things, and *especially* have photographed them.

"I've been written up as a ghost, by the way. I was riding through (Dudleytown) on my horse one time and one of those (Paranormal) groups saw me. So I just took off across a hill to go around them. Later, somebody sent me this newspaper article from Danbury (Connecticut) about the ghost on the horse. So I am one of the ghosts, I guess."[85]

I am left to wonder how many more residents are living "ghosts."

And now, after looking at the birth of the surrounding facts and genealogy of the Legend of Dudleytown, there is only one last thing to consider....how in the world did this unfortunate set of circumstances and falsehoods become a legend?

---

[85]Myers, Arthur "Is the Ghost Village of Dudleytown Really Haunted?" from <u>A Ghosthunters's Guide.</u>, 198?, Chicago, Contemporary Books. Page 53.

# The Death of a Town,
# The Birth of a Legend

*"I'm pretty convinced that the curse of Dudleytown is the ghost hunters."*[86]

NOTE: *the following contains information that comes from the two town histories already listed, and comments from residents of Cornwall who prefer not to be named. Additionally, some of the end of this chapter are my own observations based upon the entire situation.*

As previously stated, by the 1870's all the trees in and around Dudleytown, and in Cornwall, for that matter, had been cut down for the furnace's to make charcoal. Pictures of the area (only a few are left) show an area almost devoid of any trees. The trees gone, and with no crops the reason for Dudleytown's existence had vanished also. It is said that by 1880, there were fewer than 20 people left on the hill, and by 1890 less than 10.

There was a chestnut blight in 1900, and Cornwall itself was affected by it. Some historians believe that the town was almost in financial ruin because of the blight, and Dudleytown had only one--maybe two--families still living there. The trees in Dudleytown were just beginning to come back then, and it is at this time Dr. Clarke bought his land (and the next year Brophy's house would burn).

Dudleytown, then, had literally died. Was there ANY chance left for it? Not as a town, for sure. Yes, there were still one or two folk left....there are records of a Joseph Matyas, Sr., who rented some land in the South end of Dudleytown and grazed

---

[86]Ibid.

cattle.[87] No unusual occurrences were visited upon him. Some residents in the area still pick berries there, and one or two houses are occupied by locals.

After Dr. Clarke's unfortunate experience, he remarried about 1920, and just four years later formed the "Dark Entry Forest Inc.," and attempted to make The Dudleytown area a summer community, including a nature "school" for children. They built a man-made pond, and with a lot of renovations and building of summer homes for other Doctors, nurses, and lawyers. I would like for you to remember that---up till now---NO strange stories or happenings had ever been reported about Dudleytown, and as far as Dr. Clarke knew, it would be a perfect place to live.

About 12 years after his first wife's death, Dr Clarke built a brick house around 1930 on 300 acres of land just down the road from the old Tollgate, and lived there till his death in 1943. The Dark Entry Forest Inc. (DEF), had grown, and bought Bald Mountain Farm on Dudleytown Road (now Bald Mountain Road) in the 1920's as a sort of Bed and Breakfast affair to attract new members, and all seemed to be going well....and then......

They Found a Way was published in 1938. We now know what effect the book had on Dr. Clarke, but it is is unknown what effect the book had on the rest of the DEF and Cornwall. Some alive at the time state that they thought it was a quaint book, and gave no notice to it. Everyone who read it didn't believe the story of Dudleytown contained within it, as most of the other stories it contained were also embellishments. It the light of the history of the legend, apparently most of the folks that read it nation wide

---

[87]Clark, Harriet Lydia, True Facts About Dudleytown, 1989, The Cornwall Historical Society.

didn't give it much thought either. Not then, at least.

World War II came and went. Dr. Clarke died. The Korean War came and went. DEF grows somewhat, but due to the nations unfortunate troubles, not by as much as it had wanted. The trees grew strong--and very, very dense. Dark Entry Road--known for its dimness at noon at the height of the towns now dead history--regains the reason for its name. And the wildlife makes its return to the hill. All seems to be going well. Cornwall shares in the normalcy of the times also. Its population grows somewhat--though it will never break 2,000. There is only one, small (very small) problem at this time............the bugs. Then come the sixties. Cornwall attempted to end the problem of the bugs with a fix the whole nation was using----DDT. *(NOTE: what follows is hotly debated by the residents of Cornwall....some say DEF did it, others say it didn't happen at all. However, I got this bit of history from a few residents who distinctly remember it.)* It seems the town was sprayed in the late 1960's....and the Dudleytown area was sprayed HEAVILY. Too heavily, perhaps, for it seems that during most of the 1970's, and even early 80's, the wildlife was sparce in the Dudleytown area, and it was dead silent up there for most of this time.

It is also remarkable that the sixties saw the rise of Eastern Religions, which would grow up to be NEW AGE philosophy in the 70 and 80's. Additionally, during the 70's we see the resurgence of (pseudo) Satanist groups in the U.S. Anyone alive during this time will remember what I am talking about. Satanists seemed to be everywhere! And "experts" on such things appeared on all the talk shows. They even seeped into the day care centers, which were supposedly "covens" of Satanists using children in rituals. This was a time of seeming mass hysteria. Luckily, it all ended when most of the "experts" (who were promoting the whole thing) were found to be frauds. Unfortunately, though, not before a lot of innocent people were sent to jail. In the middle of all this, Ed Warren, who formed his New England Paranormal Society in 1952, became famous, and soon his Society would begin splitting and forming others. Lots of others.[88]

Ghost Hunters by the Warrens is published in the 1980's, and in the midst of the now blossoming Paranormal Groups, all looking for a place to "investigate," the legend of Dudleytown is reborn, once a simply "embellished" story in a group of unrelated stories, the ghost town grows into a target. Articles abound....seances held....and by 1993, Dan Ackroyd is saying that Dudleytown is "the most haunted place on earth."[89]

Please note that the residents of Cornwall are *very* aware of the history of Dudleytown. I have, in my possession, a school play that was written by one resident that tells the history of Dudleytown during its heyday. They are also *very* aware of the "bogus" history surrounding it too. If asked to comment on Dudleytown, some residents will become very angry, and clam up about it and brush you off. Others will make a flighting comment on it, and tell you its all false. Most will answer curtly, and change the subject. Be aware that most of these small New England towns zealously guard their privacy, and dislike *anyone* "butting" into their business. Cornwall, being a small town, acts accordingly, and if you look at the overall picture of this area of Connecticut, is *no different* than the rest of the little villages. They want to be left alone—but because of Dudleytown, drastic action had to be taken. More about this later when we talk about DEF.

---

[88]It is *estimated* that there are, or have been, over 50 "splinter groups" from the Warrens.

[89]What is odd about Mr. Ackroyd's statement in Playboy is that he seemingly does not know where it is! He says: "Dudleytown, MASSACHUSETTS"!!

Also, please note that I am reasonably certain that the authors of They Found A Way probably did *not* make up everything they wrote about. It only stands to reason that at least *some* of the stories *had* to be around before the book. So I started asking questions–and finally got some answers.

The Patterson's were a family who reportedly owned "Bonney House" in Dudleytown at one time. Some residents remember that some of them lived in a home on Route 45 not far from DEF land in the early 1900's and that no one ever saw them. They put messages in bottles outside the door and neighbors periodically picked them up and delivered the groceries or medicine the family needed. But their presence on DEF/Dudleytown land in the early part of this century definitely influenced the "everyone in DEF/Dudleytown is crazy" myth. The Patterson's were, most of the elderly residents say, insane. Some speculate that the authors of They Found A Way got their information from the Patterson's. Admittedly, this is only *hearsay* evidence. Other folks believe it was the "Raggies" who spread the idea that the area had a strange effect on people (and considering that the Raggies were foreign, always breathing and covered in charcoal, one might, at that time, tend to believe it).

But why didn't anyone stop this from getting out of hand? Why hasn't, before today, anyone told the TRUE story of Dudleytown? Why didn't someone in 1938 shoot down the shoddy research of They Found A Way?

Actually, somebody *did* try to do something about it.

In correspondence between myself and one of Dr. Clarke's living daughters, I was able to glean the following information:

Shortly after the publication of They Found a Way, Dr.

Clarke had a meeting with his lawyer. According to his daughter, the conversation into the night was close enough for her to overhear it. Dr. Clarke was so upset as to what he felt was slander and lies that he wanted to sue the authors of the book. Litigation back in the 1930's, was, however, as expensive as it is now, and his lawyer informed the Doctor that the cost would be quite high. Additionally, the authors of the book had spelled his name without the "e", had not mentioned the name of his wife, and "changed enough of the story" that it would be quite hard to prove the case. Dr. Clarke was, then, advised to let it rest. He did.[90]

There are some other reasons, however, that had an impact on the legends popularity. Let us look at some.

1. <u>They Found A Way</u> While Dr. Clarke made an attempt at stopping the book, no one else in Cornwall did. No one originally gave it notice. Who would have guessed that the story would later have such an impact on Cornwall?

2. DEF. We will look at them in depth in the next chapter. Let us say here though, that their insistence on "no comment" when it comes to their property, while definitely within their rights (and I really can not blame them), *has* hurt them. Secrecy about *anything* hurts a cause, no matter how noble. For instance, I am a Freemason. Our fraternity used to maintain a "don't talk, don't tell" attitude about everything. Most people now believe we are a secret society doing all sorts of strange rituals–no matter what we now say about it, or how many charitable things we do (like donate an estimated one million dollars a day to various causes, the biggest being the Shriner's Hospitals for Children). Believe it or not, there are *still* people out there who think Masons are out to take over the

---

[90] I would hasten to say that he could have succeeded if the case would have been brought to trial today.

74

world! Nothing we can say or do now will change some minds. The damage has been done.

The DEF is the same way. Their silence *has* hurt them. It may never go away. You see, when people ask you a question, silence is *always* perceived to be an *affirmative* answer.

On the other hand, the public's *gross* disregard for their rights and privacy can not be passed off. Camera crews, biker clubs, wiccans, satanists, and more Paranormal Groups than "Carter has little pills" has tramped upon the Dudleytown area (*despite the very obvious "PRIVATE PROPERTY" signs* ) so badly that vandalism has all but ruined a historic site. While I dislike the fact that they had to close their property off, I can not blame them.

3. Cornwall. Yes, the town that Dudleytown actually resides in plays a part here. Throughout its history, Cornwall has done virtually nothing to combat the obviously false history concerning a part of their town. Even its own area newspaper speaks of the "supposedly infamous" area without so much as a reply.[91] Some have answered that the reason is that Dudleytown is *not* their land, and the Cornwall Historical Society *has* some published material to deal with it. That is true. However, the material the C.H.S. continues to publish contains gross historical mistakes–even in one written by a former curator of the Society. In it, the author still states that the Dudley brothers were returning from the French and Indian War (before the war even happened), and that, in my mind, is inexcusable. You would think that more *HISTORICAL* research would have been done to counter the terribly inaccurate "histories"

---

[91]The treatment of the fire in the Dudleytown area in 1999 is a prime example. Local newspapers had the headline "DUDLEYTOWN FIRE" and actually mentioned the Legend.

that are published about a section of their town.[92]

4. Paranormal Groups and writers. From the Warrens' "New England Society for Paranormal Research" to the new "societies," most of these groups, who exist to supposedly "study" paranormal activity, have spread the word about the legend of Dudleytown without so much as a peek at the facts. Both the "societies," and the authors of books about "Ghost Towns," etc, with the exception of the Warrens, have taken *carte blanche* the version of the legend in They Found a Way and profligate it. The Warrens version of the legend is so different as to be counted as fiction, with virtually none of their story able to be verified or researched. The sole exception to all of this is Authur Myers, who, in his book A Ghosthunters's Guide, shows that he took the time to travel to the area, interview some knowledgeable residents, and seems to be aware of the problems with the legend[93].

All of the above, some understandable, some not, converged to form a thorn that, to this day, is firmly embedded in the side of a sleepy little New England town, one that has no idea how to heal itself.

Just as I was finishing up this chapter, an amazing thing happened. I had thought that the book was done, and was about to believe it would only be a short, 80 page or so booklet. There was

---

[92]To their credit, some members of the Society are now aware of the inaccuracies in their files, and are working to correct them.

[93]Before you begin thinking that ALL Paranormal Groups are misinformed, I wish to state that some of them are quite serious in their desire to actually study their subject. Additionally, of late many are supporting DEF efforts to keep undesirables off Dudleytown (DEF) land in a sincere effort to have it reopened, and even assist in maintaining it.

one thing I *really* wanted, but thought that I would never get: I wanted to actually talk to a real, live, member of Dark Entry Forest, Inc. I had already known that the corporation would not grant interviews or statements to anyone, but prayed that maybe one or two would speak on their own. Then it happened.

One day in my email box was a letter from one of their members! While the person agreed to answer a few questions, I was warned that the person's name should not be used. I readily agreed.

Then a true miracle occurred. Apparently a few other members of DEF knew about my website, and wanted to make a few statements also. One member said: "It is time that something was said."

Another was Dr. Clarkes' daughter. I was originally told that Lydia (her name) would not speak on any topic about Dudleytown. I was happy to find that not only would she speak, but provided most of the insight included in this book concerning her father's relation, not only to Dudleytown, but also DEF.

We will now turn to the most controversial aspect of the modern Dudleytown legend–a group that some say is as mysterious as the legend itself. Most people will tell you they are hiding something, or worse yet protecting something.

The truth is, they are, and what it is just may surprise you.

# The D.E.F.

*"We don't mind people writing about the place if they don't entice other people to come and visit."*[94]

No investigation into Dudleytown would be complete without mentioning Dark Entry Forest, Inc. (DEF), most normally referred to as the Dark Entry Forest Association, although it was *never* an "Association," but instead a corporation. This "cabal" like group (visitors words, not mine) owns 850 acres of land that includes all of Dudleytown, encompassing what is now know as the "Bonney Brook Watershed." What most visitors to the area will mention is that DEF "forces" people to leave the Dudleytown area, and are very close-mouthed. It is said that they tow cars away after dark, forbid people from going certain places near Dudleytown, and act as their own police force in the area. Some residents say that it is an exclusive "rich peoples" club. Many will also say that DEF are all "demon-possessed", and others that DEF *knows* that Dudleytown is haunted and are trying to protect people. So what is the truth?

Because DEF *is* very closed-mouthed about itself, a *true* a look at them is very hard to get. However, in talking to many residents of Cornwall and members of DEF (those that would speak to me), there does seem to be an animosity between the town and the corporation. Just how bad that animosity is I was not able to determine. Be that as it may, some published materials of DEF are still in existence, and I have a few examples of them. Here are the facts that I have been able to determine:

Dark Entry Forest, Inc., was incorporated on December 9, 1924, by Lucius F. Robinson, Francis W. Cole, and Lucius F.

---

[94]John Leich, former President of the Dark Entry Forest. Inc., quoted in MYERS, page 48.

Robinson, Jr (all of Hartford, Ct).[95] They were attorneys presumably acting for the members of DEF, who seemed to not be present at the signing. The Corporation was to sell $100,000 worth of stock, divided into 1,000 shares. Members were to buy 10 shares of that stock for $100 each, and that limited the DEF to no more than 100 members. At the time of the incorporation, $1,000 was a *lot* of money. It seems that the members were to be invited in at first.

All of the original members, according to the people whom I spoke to, were doctors, lawyers, and nurses whom Doctor William Clarke knew. In fact, that one of the streams in the area is known as "Five Nurses Creek." There is no doubt in anyone's mind that the original intention was for the Dudleytown/Bonney Brook Watershed to be a "get away" (DEF member prefer the term "pastoral escape") for New York Doctors and Nurses–at least at first.

DEF's first meeting was February 9th, 1926, at which 41 members were present. Dr. William C. Clarke and his new wife Carita were among those attending, and most of the other members were professional people also.

So far, all that we have been told concerning DEF in the past is true. A short set of by-laws, typical of any newly formed corporation, is included with the certificate of incorporation, and is not remarkable. Apparently none of the 41 new members thought anything was amiss on their newly acquired land.

An advertising pamphlet was mailed out about this time with a short history of DEF and its property, written by Dr. Clarke,

---

[95]Certificate of Incorporation of Dark Entry Forest, Inc. dated December 9, 1924.

along with a membership application. Another pamphlet went out on April 1, 1931, along with the same short history (it is quoted in the Prelude to this book) and it reveals that many of the plans of the DEF had expanded. It now appeared to be a resort-like organization that included: Bald Mountain Farm, which was restored with some plumbing and electricity, and provided sleeping for 15 and dining room for 20; The Bee Hive House, with sleeping for 12 and a well equipped kitchen; and the Warren Road House, at the foot of the hill, which was rented out to non-members (with hopes of making them members). Be aware that those houses (Bald Mountain Farm, the Bee Hive, and the Warren Road House) are the *only* houses still standing from the Dudleytown days. Most folks believe that they are about 200 years old. Included in DEF's holdings were a few members cabins, and three over-night camps. Cabin sites were available for $10 per year. Additionally, a "summer school" for children of the members and to be taught by the more scholarly of the adult members would teach the ideal of forest conservation to the youngsters. Swimming places were within easy reach of the summer folks, and so was horseback riding and skiing in the winter! Additionally, there were now *different* classes of membership, including an "honorary" one.[96]

If you hadn't guessed, it was plainly stated in the 1931 brochure that "life in the open, in relation to the life in the forest," was the main ideal of DEF.[97] A members list included with the pamphlet listed Dr. Clarke, who had been on the Board of Directors from 1926-1931, his wife, and three children. Nothing in the pamphlet mentions ghosts, demons, or anything out of the ordinary. In fact, it is made out to be a place of beauty. All their advertising

---

[96]Membership today seems to be a two or three year affair. You apply, and wait. The entire DEF must then vote upon your application.

[97]Dark Entry Forest, Inc., 1931.

80

said that the beauty, and the solitude, would last forever. Unfortunately, again, like in the legend, the bad times came.....

In 1938 They Found A Way was published, and it appears that Dr. Clarke was the only member of DEF to attempt to do anything about the book. There are no other mentions of it in DEF material to my, or other members of DEF's, knowledge.

Dr. Clarke died in 1943, and not much is known that is of interest from 1943 to the present. DEF is still in operation, of course, and is still using a few of the buildings to recruit new members. The woods are still there, and so is most of the wildlife. So why all the fuss?

When the "curse" stories became popular, the "ghost hunters" began to arrive. Not realizing, at first, at least, that the land of their quest was owned, they began intruding on the life of DEF members still living there. Understand, here are folks who have bought membership in a select community, favoring the solitude of the wilderness, enjoying life, and then someone comes walking in their back yard and tells them that the land that they own is haunted! Add to that the fact the area *is* dangerous enough to walk on during the day, and then to do it at night? Many DEF members just knew a law suit was coming.

So DEF did what they had to: they fought back. Not a real fight, mind you, but all they could do. They denied that Dudleytown was haunted. They started towing cars parked overnight. They tried changing the name of Dudleytown Road to

Bald Mountain Road.[98] They posted signs. Troop B of the Connecticut State Police was asked to patrol more often–especially at night. The town occasionally cooperated, an example being The Cornwall Historical Society, who printed hand-outs to those who inquired of them about Dudleytown.

Some of this worked, but unfortunately not all of it did, especially as time went on and new "wrenches" were cast into the machine. Although it is now well known that the bulk of what was Dudleytown is private property, the "ghost hunters", and others out for a thrill, still trod on the land. The original ideal of DEF still lingered. They used to allow hikers during the day (so long as they stayed on the trails), and warn all of the inherent dangers of the area.

Year after year, more and more people came, first alone or with a friend or two, then in groups, and finally in buses. That's right, *buses.* The Connecticut police, Troop B in Canann, reported one, and residents speak of at least *three* being up there (not all at one time, though). They came during the day, and especially at night when it was the "spookiest", and even more on Halloween night. The area started looking shabby–vandalism was the order of the day. Even the occupied houses on Bald Mountain Road were not immune. Some residents reported tools, lawn decorations, and other things missing. A few folks reported "groups" of people *in*

---

[98]There is a little controversy over the street name. It is a fact that at the beginning of Dudleytown, the name *was* Dudleytown Road from one side of the hill to the other. If you look at a map, it still does. Apparently, during the 1860-1880 time period it became Bald Mountain Road. When the town added street signs, they were surprised to find the name of their street was now Dudleytown Road South. The DEF membership (according to most) changed back to Bald Mountain during the 1960's to stop the flow of traffic into the newly haunted (!) area. This is, at least, the consensus of the residents.

*their yards.* While Cornwall may have occasionally helped to discourage these "visitors," other towns and people did not. I have an flyer that was produced by a neighboring town that is promoting a "play" about the "history" of Dudleytown. The play was produced *without* Cornwall or DEF's knowledge or participation. Additionally, Paranormal groups freely passed out directions to Dudleytown, and "experts" Ed and Loraine Warren gave lectures that included their version of the Dudleytown legend, along with directions posted on their website.

DEF then began discussing other methods of combating the influx of visitors, but right after the release of the movie "The Blair Witch Project," things got drastic. Most of the residents state that "visits" to Dudleytown increased dramatically, as many actually believed that the movie was *based* on Dudleytown (it wasn't, the movie was totally fabricated), and wanted to "experience" the horror.

While the town as a whole, along with DEF, points to these things as justification for the measures it took most people do not believe them, I happen to know that they were real. During this time I received scores of email letters from people who actually bragged about going up to Dudleytown with friends with the sole intention of scarring each other. One such letter spoke of the person donning a hockey mask and taking a machete to play "Jason" from the "Friday the 13th" movies and actually bragged that he "scared the hell" out of his girlfriend. God must have been merciful, for no one was hurt–at least that time. Had the visits increased any more, there was no telling what would happen.

The summer of 1999 saw a fire in Dudleytown. It is always dangerous during the summers there, and that year it was especially dry. Lightning hit, and within a short time four acres were gone. That did not stop the vandals though, for while all the newspapers reported the fire accurately, some saw it as part of the "curse." A radio diskjockey then violated the area by doing a broadcast *right from Dudleytown*, as if to "dare" the curse.[99] More and more people started coming, and the area became more and more vandalized. One well known Monroe, Connecticut "Paranormal Investigator" was removed from Dudleytown with his camera crew, who was apparently filming an "investigation." He cursed and swore that Dudleytown was public property.

In September 1999, DEF had all it could take, and it voted to close the Dudleytown/DEF property area to the public, and posted "NO TRESPASSING" signs along all the borders of their land, and informed the Connecticut State Troopers to take appropriate action on anyone they found. Within the first month, approximately 29 citations were issued.

Within two days after the closure, over a hundred email letters flooded my computer mailbox: "why did they do that?" and "what did *you* tell them that made them close it" (as if I personally knew everyone in DEF, or was a member myself) were common, but the majority read like this:

"What a shame a few immature people would ruin it for everyone else. I love to walk in that area, and now its gone."

"What idiots! I used to go there for *years*, and now its shut down! Can't you get a membership or something? There *must* be something that can be done!"

And still others:

---

[99] At least that is the story that was broadcast! In truth, the DJ did his show from the *bottom* of the hill, and saved himself a trespassing arrest!

"If *only* they would open it up to everyone. That would *prove* to people that it isn't haunted"

That sentiment has been repeated by quite a number of people. If DEF would *just* open the area, build a museum, perhaps restore a few of the old cellar holes and build houses on them, then much of the "draw" of the area would disappear. I don't really think so. It didn't stop Salem, Massachusetts from being a tourist town, and it didn't detract from the Amityville House (still getting about 100 "drive-by's" per week!). There is no reason to believe it would stop the "ghost hunters" from coming to Dudleytown either.

Why should they open it up? It is their land. They bought it *for* the solitude. They *had* it opened during the day, when it was safe, for years...and for their thanks the land was trashed. And what would make anyone think that opening it up would stop the belief that Dudleytown is haunted? Facts haven't stopped them. My Website didn't.

And this book probably will not either.

Unfortunately, there may be no answer to their dilemma.

Luckily, just before the land was closed, I finally had a chance to visit Dudleytown.

# My Trip to Dudleytown

*"Dad, what's so special about THIS place?"* [100]

My wife and I left on vacation on the 25th of June, 1999, at 5 a.m. from San Antonio and drove to Nashville arriving late in the evening. There were a number of reasons for going, first and foremost being that my wife had Leukemia, and wanted to see our grandson Kyle before her bone marrow transplant in September. The next morning we left at 6 a.m. and arrived at my son's house at about 7 p.m. (2,000 miles in 2 days! Not bad for an old man!) My son lived in Glasboro, New Jersey, at the time, and as his wife is a Funeral Director, the house was–you guessed it--a Funeral Home! (Should that have set the stage for the visit to Dudleytown? I think so!)

On June 30th, we left for Cornwall (remember now, Dudleytown was not a real town) about eight o'clock in the morning, and arrived at our meeting point in Kent at about 11:30. There, we were to meet our guides (whom I am happy to say are our friends) Nancy Ziegler and the famously infamous Robin Barron. In addition, Catherine Pond, a freelance writer, joined us. Nancy and Barron are both members of the Cosmic Society for Paranormal Investigation--but for the record, they were *not* acting on behalf of the group, they were just doing us a *large* favor by leading us up there. I am glad they did. As you will see, the trip *could* have been either disastrous, boring, or at the least unsafe if you do not know what you are doing or looking for.

As the wife and I were parched, we had arranged to meet everyone at a small Italian restaurant behind the train depot in Kent, and proceeded to down 2-3 glasses of Iced Tea while making

---

[100] This was my son's reaction when he first saw Dudleytown on our trip.

all the usual introductions and small talk. Barron then placed two large volumes of pictures on the table, and showed us the many interesting and strange things they had witnessed in

Nancy "Raz" Zeigler and Robin Barron at Dark Entry Road. Notice the curve of the road going up. It gets steeper, too!

Dudleytown, setting the stage for our journey. We left for Cornwall after about an hour, and arrived at Dark Entry Road. Cornwall is about nine miles *north* of Kent, and for those of you who are wondering, yes, Dark Entry Road *does* have a street sign. Conveniently, there is a parking area about 10 feet from it!

Should DEF ever open up Dudleytown again, let me say quickly--NEVER, *EVER*, attempt to walk up Dark Entry at night! It was hard enough for me by day, as it is a hike up a HILL---hard, rocky ground--and it would be *more* than dangerous at night. In fact, it would be totally crazy! Its paved for about half of it--the rest is the stony ground. As there are no signs either directing or pointing to anything or anywhere, you *have* to know what you are looking for. If you do not know what to look for, then just hope you

87

see some of the cellar holes. Which, by the way, along with the stone walls, are all that there is to see. Now on to my story.

Dark Entry "Road". This is the unpaved portion

Having arrived, we gathered in the parking area and had a word of prayer (my request--I never do anything without it), and the girls separated and opted to drive up the alternate entry route–Dudleytown Road--now known as Bald Mountain Road. The advantages of Bald Mountain Road is that you can almost drive right into what is left of Dudleytown. The disadvantage is that all the residents see you coming, and there is only room for one vehicle to park and if it is not gone by dusk it gets towed--no questions asked! Again, no matter which way you go, if you do NOT know what you are looking for, you won't see anything! Anyway, up went my son, Barron, me, and a friend of Nancy and Barron's named Craig, armed with video and still cameras to record the journey, and capture anything we saw.

If nothing else, this trip taught me that I am seriously out of shape! Barron, in his 60's, put me to shame! About a quarter of a mile up Dark Entry there is a tree that is jutting out from the left side of the road in a very odd shape. Barron called it the "Hound of the Dudleyvilles," and I must admit it does look like a dog. A little further is a tree bulging at the base that Barron said we should all pat for good luck. I blessed it. Then, because I was so out of breath from the walk, I patted it anyway! (hey, its now blessed, so who did it hurt?) Farther up, there is a Ranger's house, and across from it what was identified as a celebrities summer home (no, I will not tell you the name, and most wouldn't guess it anyway. That it belongs to a celebrity was later denied by a local). We bothered neither of the folks, and crossed a tree blocking the road. At that point the pavement ended and the stony ground began. (I was later told that the paved area was public road, and where the pavement ends marks the beginning of DEF property)

The "Hound of the Dudleyvilles"

Three things need to be said, and in one case restated. First, it was readily apparent why the road was called Dark Entry. The trees *were* really so thick that the road was dim all the way up---and it was *past* noon! Secondly, after the road ended, unless you had on hiking boots, you might as well have forgotten it. I wore Air Force issued Alaskan Combat boots, and it was still rough! You MUST be careful up there! Thirdly, while the trees were dense, you could tell that most of the trees were less than 100 years old. Remember the history of the place--they were all cut down for the charcoal burners during the 1800's. We heard birds chirping, and saw a little wildlife all the way. (so, unfortunately, there goes the "silence all the time" statements I kept hearing about!)

Up we went, with me stopping every once in awhile to videotape the journey. Barron pointed out two supposed meeting places that witches met in for their rituals. While no hard evidence for this was present, I could see the possibilities of that. We crossed a dam (actually, we went right through it). This dam, I believe, was made for one of the mills that were in the area during the high point of Dudleytown's existence. It has been dubbed "witches dam" by our guides. It is actually named "Marsella Falls", and appears so on the maps of the area. After about an hours hike, we arrived at the junction of Dudleytown and Dark Entry Roads. There were *no* signs marking the junction, and if you do not look for it, you would never know. We had arrived in Dudleytown!

I was in history heaven, and the MECCA OF PARANORMAL ACTIVITY!! The "most haunted place on earth." What did I think??

What I thought was: "where did they get all these damn mosquitoes?"

You have to understand--I am a mosquito magnet......want to get rid of yours? Invite me over---they love me! Luckily, Nancy and Barron brought about 15 million cans of "Off" and several other repellants, and after a period of spraying, we were "off" exploring!

I spotted about 5 cellar holes (I was told it was "bad Karma" to go into them, but yes, into them I went). For your information, these are actually "root cellars." They were a common feature of many early American houses, and were designed to keep the harvest preserved. A well designed one could maintain temperatures 20 to 40 degrees lover than outside temperatures during the summer, and above freezing during the winter. Additionally, their were numerous stone walls. Some of the walls are placed in such a way that you can tell they were built to enclose something---probably livestock, or for designating boundaries (for the charcoal burners or mills). The birds continued to chirp, the chipmunks continued to scurry, and the mosquitoes continued to bite. We continued to explore. There were a few more odd tree formations--one had a rather large opening in it that you could see through. It was a beautiful place--I loved it.

Then came the "Vortex." The "Vortex," as it has been explained to me, is the *CENTER* of the weird stuff in Dudleytown. Everyone, it seems, experiences something there. What it *really* is, is Cook Road (see map). My wife, Catherine, and I couldn't wait! Nancy said that she would rather stay out, and Craig wasn't sure. I said "COOL, LETS GO," and proceeded in. We stopped after about 15 minutes of walking, as I was just plain worn out by 3 hours of steady hiking. Not to mention that nothing had happened. Well, that's not quite true. Catherine and I got 3 more Mosquito bites for our troubles. And the birds were continuing to chirp. I did, however, get suitable videotape of the journey, and Craig (also armed with a video camera, did also.

As the "Vortex" was only about 5 minutes from Dudleytown Road, where the girls had parked the car, we returned there and went down the hill the easy way. Barron, my son, and Craig hiked back down Dark Entry (Barron had lost his hat band). The hike back was much easier, they said (I bet it was!).

91

We journeyed into Cornwall and looked at the remains of the old Missionary school--which is right next to the 1st Congregational church. The Missionary school was were David Carter went when he returned to "civilization." You will read about that in the next chapter. We then returned to Kent for a well needed supper!

Did I see any ghosts? While we were in Kent eating, I rewound my video camera for a look at the tape. We all held our breath, wondering if anything "special" would show up. Other than me almost tripping over some stones in one scene (my wife's favorite part), nothing.

I really didn't expect to. But think about this--A DUDLEY in DUDLEYTOWN. If there was any "curse" on the Dudley name, I should have been a prime target. So was I disappointed? NO! I loved it! And if I am in the area again, and the DEF opens it back up, I *will* return!

Just not at night!

# A Few Loose Ends
### "Where are they now....?"

*Note: the following material comes from Starr's History, and town, state, and other local histories.*

So what became of some of the other legend mentioned Dudleytown inhabitants? Did they die mysterious deaths or had weird things happen to them? Who bought their houses afterwards, and did anything happen to the new inhabitants?

Gideon and Barzillai, as mentioned before, are currently lost to us. As more of Connecticut's records become available, this slight mystery will be solved. Gideon, as mentioned, was in his sixties when he left. I would suspect that he did not live long afterwards.

As for Gideon Dudley's house, Captain Andrew Andrews bought it and raised two sons: Benajah, who became an attorney in Middletown; and Andre, who became a Major in the Army and served in the Revolutionary War, later a States Attorney, and afterwards practiced Law in Buffalo, New York, where he died of Cholera. A Captain Thorp was the last owner of the house. He went west.

As mentioned, Abiel Dudley died at the age of 90, and is buried in the Cornwall Cemetery in an unmarked grave (typical for paupers at the time). William Tanner died at 104 years in the house of his widowed daughter. He is also buried in Cornwall, with a very prominent headstone. Both men died naturally of old age.

John T. Andrew–he who built the stone wall in Dudleytown–studied for the ministry, but had throat trouble and could not preach. It was *then* he built the stone wall (and many say *most* of the stone walls in Dudleytown were either built by, or the

93

building of them were supervised by, him). He later took a great interest in Cornwall's schools, and was a writer on agricultural subjects. He died naturally.

The Jones family. The family itself was descended from Lt. Gov. Jones of the New Haven Colony. Zechariah Howe Jones held various Cornwall offices, and his father Caleb (whom took Abiel Dudley for a year) became a much respected teacher. Samuel Jones was Mayor of Cornwall, and was grandfather to Samuel Jones Tilden–who is granted a unique place in history. Born in New York, he later went on to fight corruption in that state against William M. "Boss" Tweed. But his inclusion in history was ensured when we ran for President of the United States against Rutherford B. Hayes in 1876. Although Tilden won 250,000 more *popular* (cast) votes than Hayes, the *electoral* votes were contested in several states. The Electoral Commission of 1877 created by Congress declared Hayes the winner by one electoral vote, and Tilden retired from public life. He bequeathed most of his fortune for the establishment of the New York Public Library upon his death.

Thomas Porter, a Deacon in the Cornwall church, became a Captain in the Army, served in the Revolutionary War, was a selectman of the town, and later a Judge of the Vermont Supreme Court. His son Ebenezer, who was *born* in Dudleytown, became President of Andover Seminary. They both died naturally.

And now the Carters.....those unfortunate folks who moved from Dudleytown and killed by the Indians. Here, for the first time, is the complete story.[101]

---

[101]This information comes from a variety of sources, including *The History of Goshen*, historical articles, and living descendants.

## The Legend of Dudleytown

It is 1763, the last year of the French/Indian War. The Carters, along with two other families (one named Duncan), moved to the "Forks of the Delaware", and clear some land near the bank of the river and build a house which would lodge the three families.

One October morning, Nathaniel Carter and the two other men left to do some work. A party of twelve Indians, who had been watching while the men left, let out screams and rushed upon the women and children in the house. The description of the massacre is given in gruesome detail in the "Legend" found in this (and other) books, and, for many of them, is the only thing is does report accurately–and therefore I will not repeat it. Elizabeth Carter, who had been just a few feet from the door, was immediately taken prisoner. Mother Carter, the baby, and two girls who had been sick in bed were immediately killed. During the attack, one of the men heard the screams and returned. He got off one shot before he died.

The Indians (most of the histories say they were Cherokee) returned to their encampment (consisting of about 200), with the three Carter children, two children belonging to another family, and Mrs. Duncan. Elizabeth escaped during the first nights and returned to her destroyed home. Becoming overly distraught, however, she was easily recaptured.

Meanwhile Nathaniel Carter and Mr. Duncan returned home to find the desolation, and ran to the nearest white settlement and obtained help. They returned to their burnt-out home just in time to meet a full war party of braves–and were scalped.

The captives all stayed with the Indians for a while, and lived with the Cherokee in Canada until finally the two Carter girls were ransomed near Ft. Niagara. The other captives were all eventually either ransomed or were let go at the end of the war.

So what happened to the children? It is generally believed that Sarah was so affected by the experience that she was confined to an asylum. Elizabeth married Benjamin Oviatt, and had many children before her death at 79 years of age–and her descendants are living today. That leaves the son.........

Young Nathanial Carter married an Indian girl, and died at about 70 years of age. He had a son, named David C. Carter--whose Indian name most say was Ta-wah. He eventually attended the Indian Mission School in Cornwall![102] The school had been started in 1816 to train "foreign" youth to become schoolmasters and missionaries, and to help those youth communicated culture and civilization "among the heathen nations."

Well, things were not so politically correct back then as they are now, and when David (or Ta-wah, if you like) and his friends Elias Boudinot and John Ridge, started giving three of the local Cornwall girls the eye, the town got upset. When David wanted to actually *marry* one, things got downright ugly, and David was apparently "dismissed with censure" in 1825.

So he wound up in abject poverty, a victim of the Dudleytown curse, right? David Carter became a journalist, an editor of the "Cherokee Advocate" newspaper, and was appointed a Chief Justice of the Supreme Court of the Cherokee Nation, *and their Delegate to Congress.* He died at Tahlequah, Indian Territories, on January 6, 1867. He and his wife had 11 children.

What happened to the school? It was disbanded in 1827. Apparently, it had done its job too well.

---

[102]Just for your information, the ruins of the Mission School still stand in Cornwall, and, *yes*, it is said to be haunted. By who or what, however, nobody seems to know.

## The Legend of Dudleytown

With all the naturalness of the deaths that occurred in Dudleytown, and the successes of those who lived there, we are left to wonder: *What curse?*

That does, of course, bring us right back to the beginning. I stated in the Preface that after the facts started coming in, I wished to find out the "why" regarding the legend. I have *not* been able to do that. Explain the legend as false, yes. State what *really* happened, yes. Prove my point, definitely. Explain how the legend became so widespread and popular despite the fact that *nothing* really happened, no. The legend of Dudleytown ranks right up there with the "legends" regarding George Washington and the cherry tree, or his throwing a coin across the Potomac. Or, even, that the Civil War was fought to free the slaves.

People just *want* to believe it, no matter what. Unfortunately, unlike the historical things I just mentioned, the legend of Dudleytown *continues* to affect the town of Cornwall and the members of DEF. It impacts their lives, and may *never* go away.

# Afterword

Luckily, the main body of my research ended about September, 1999, for the next month my wife lost her battle with Leukemia. Before her death, I tried various times to get a book published on Dudleytown, but one publisher would say "too weird for us", and another "not weird enough for us," or some words to that effect.

After my wife's death, I had no desire for a while to go on with the book. My friends, however, kept encouraging me to continue with the plans, and also to finish another volume of my genealogical series. The latter project, on the Concord branch of the Dudley family, was finished in May of 2000. I then decided to try another approach for the Dudleytown story.

Most genealogists I spoke to were fascinated by my story about Dudleytown. Finally, one said: "Hey, you solved this mystery by using genealogy, so why not write the book that way. I am *sure* other genealogists will look at this differently that other people." I was sure he was right. Another said: "try an article first, see if someone will take it." And I did. I wrote a letter to Heritage Quest magazine proposing an article about Dudleytown with just that in mind–showing how genealogical and historical research could solve historical mysteries. They accepted it. I sent a copy of the article to Heritage Books, Inc., my genealogical publisher, and proposed that I rewrite the Dudleytown book as an expansion of the article, slanted to tell the story of my research on it. They accepted the book. The article was published in the September/October issue of Heritage Quest. You are reading the book.

Fellow genealogists, our noble hobby can do so much if we only open our minds to the possibilities. Actually, we go about our searches in the exact same way many historians do, if not in *more* depth than they do. Think about it!

While this book took a look at something *paranormal*, it ended up telling me a great deal about what one branch of the family went through to survive. It also explained a lot about local legends. I could not pay a college enough to teach me what my hobby did about the early history of our nation. Even my history classes benefitted by this.

We can use our talents to research *anything* we want. We look for, and find, things even some historians don't. *We* know where to look to find out things about people, and places. *We* know how to solve jigsaw puzzles that would give others headaches. *If* only we would use it more! If nothing else, and if you gained nothing else by reading this humble tome, know that with the knowledge you have of genealogy, you can do anything you want.

God Bless.

# And in Conclusion...
## Frequently asked questions about Dudleytown

Somewhere during all this research some people started calling me an "expert" on Dudleytown. I am not. Some of it came about, I am sure, due to both of my web pages and my interviews with various newspapers on the East Coast, my article in Heritage Quest Magazine, and my genealogical books. While calling me an "expert" gives a great boost to my male ego, I am totally convinced that two hours after this book goes to press I will find at least three things I should have added. Worse yet, I will probably find a mistake!

However, there are a few last words (really! This is the end!) in response to questions that I always get asked about Dudleytown that I would like to address.

People usually ask me if the Legend of Dudleytown is a myth, a legend, or just a ghost story. The answer is: its an Legend. Ghost stories have only a cursory basis in fact. That is, usually only *one* thing (sometimes two) will have any relevance to something real. Additionally, ghost stories are usually *contemporary*, that is, they are usually not very old in relation to the present. You will ask: what about *historical ghost stories?* Didn't I refer to them in the beginning? Yes, I did. That is because the term is something most people could relate to. Additionally, and here is the ONE thing that differentiates them from a Legend. *Ghost stories contain ghosts.* Dudleytown does *NOT.* Yes, I said it does NOT contain ghosts. Read "The Legend of Dudleytown" again. No ghosts. Also, ghost stories *explain* nothing. They just exist. They are there for entertainment only.

A myth, of course, is not based upon fact, and are plainly fanciful tales. The dictionary defines it as: "a fictitious idea."

Legends *are* based upon fact, or at least factual places and/or people. They are stories that contain names, places, and/or things that people will recognize because *something* in them, or of them, is still around. The dictionary says "a traditional tale that explains beliefs, practices, or natural phenomena, many times based on fact or history." All of Dudleytown's history is recorded–*even in the Legend.* That no one has checked the facts, and that some of the Legend is totally false is a moot point right now. Also, the story of Dudleytown *does* try to explain why the area is deserted, and it *has* affected people–an entire town. The time for the Legend to be faced and explored has come. We can only hope that it ends.

So now, the book is at an end. *YOU* now know the facts. Wether or not you chose to believe them is entirely up to you.

# Frequently asked questions about Dudleytown

*The following are the most frequently asked questions about Dudleytown from my web site.*

1. So there is NO link from Robert Dudley, Earl of Leicester, to the Dudleytown brothers?

Correct--there is none. I have only a slight idea as to how anyone may have gotten this--but as it involves genealogy, a science that most of the Legend tellers have no knowledge of, I seriously doubt that it would have figured in. The link appears to be totally fabricated, and is NOT supported by history or genealogy.

2. When was Dudleytown founded?

In 1737, when Thomas Griffis purchased the land at an Auction. It became known as Dudleytown after the three Dudley brothers--Gideon, Barzillai, and Abiel, settled there.

3. So there was only THREE brothers--not 4?

Correct. Martin Dudley, NOT connected to the Dudleytown brothers, arrived later. He married Gideon's daughter Anna in Cornwall. LaFayette arrived much later, and again was from another branch of the family.

4. Are you saying that Dudleytown was NEVER a town--it never had even a church?

Correct. Dudleytown was, and is, part of Cornwall. It was never incorporated as a town. It only had about 20 houses on the hill at any one time. No churches, cemeteries, meeting houses, or things like that. Its population never exceeded 100, and most historians put the number far below--about 50.

5. You state that all the deaths there are natural. What do you have to support this?

Town records, histories of Cornwall, obituaries, church records, letters from residents (those still in existence) were all used in this work. I have evidence for every one of the deaths. Everything you need to check the deaths are given here in the book.

6. Then why do people say they are all part of a "curse?" Surely they can't all be lying!

I have no earthly idea why "they" say that. As stated earlier, the first "Dudleytown is haunted" story was written in 1938 in a book They Found A Way. I have no idea where they got their information. Everyone else seems to have copied, and embellished, the original.

7. Do you really believe Dr. Clark, whose wife went mad in the last happening, REALLY bought the town?

No, I KNOW it. Dr. Clarke, along with other Doctors and friends, bought *the entire 850 acres* and founded the "Dark Entry Forest, Inc.," who own it today.

8. But what about all the photographs of Dudleytown? The ones with all the ghosts in them? Are they forgeries?

I cannot say that. The pictures at my Web Site are from the SAME trip that are on another Site that has "energy globules," "snakes" etc. There are none in mine, but many in theirs. I can not help but wonder why. The things (now watch what I say) that are in their photo's CAN be faked, or attributed to lens flare, cigarette smoke, or just fog. I will just have to leave the truthfulness of the ghost pictures on the Internet to you to decide. As you can see, the photo's in this book have *no* ghosts in them.

9. But I was up there! I *felt* something! How do you explain THAT?

I could try: You went up there *expecting* something. You went into what even I admit is a spooky looking place--all cold and forested. You probably went with others who believed in it, and guess what? You experienced something!

And that is the main problem with all "psychic" experiences....and the main reason why the Paranormal Sciences will never be taken seriously as a *science*. It relies on *emotion* and experience, not facts or tangible evidence. People *feel* things everyday--but never act upon them or draw conclusions from them. With "ghosts", however, it seems to be different.

10. So YOU do not believe in the Paranormal, right?

On the contrary--I do. But only that which can be reasonably proven. I must know the background of what I am shown. As a historian, and a genealogist, I deal in FACTS. I research what I can, and *then* draw conclusions from what I find, and then from what I see. Some folks have what is called "confirmation bias." That is, they *only* use what "facts" will *prove* their case, and discard all others. I do not. I will use the most reliable information that *can be proven*, and if necessary, I *will* change my mind. That is how this book came to be. At first, I *believed* that there could be something to this Legend. *FACTS* changed my mind.

11. But I just *know* you are wrong.

There is one simple way to disprove me. Research my facts. Do *not* just believe me. *Find out for yourself.* I did it in Texas--and so can you, wherever you are!

12. Yea, and those OWLS! I was up there, and didn't see ANYTHING!

Lucky you. There are bears, snakes, bobcats, and assorted other goodies in Dudleytown. And lots of birds. You didn't stay the night (I know, because it is not allowed, and they tow cars there after dusk). However, residents (of which I do know a few) report wildlife everywhere. Do remember, we humans tend to make a lot of noise, which our animal friends just do not like!

13. But people keep telling me its DEAD silent!

When I was there, there were birds chirping, we saw a chipmunk, and everything was as a forest should be. Others have told me the same thing. I would imagine that those who had heard nothing probably scarred the wildlife away.

14. How can you use HISTORY to prove a PARANORMAL thing? And what IS GENEALOGY?

Because history is based upon FACTS. Paranormal experiences are just that–an experience, something someone *believes* happened to them. Ghosts (if you believe in them) occur because of *something*: their life wasn't complete; they died without finishing something; they had an terrible thing happen to them, etcetera. Whatever. The HISTORY of Dudleytown shows that none of this ever occurred there. In fact, *many* of the deaths connected to Dudleytown never even took place there! Do the math............80% of the legend of Dudleytown is *false*–made up! Another 15% is pure embellishment---that is, something that DID happen that was expanded, and added to. Sort of like the Blair Witch Project--a mythology that many get sucked into and believed in, and it is false.

GENEALOGY is the study of ones ancestors---your roots! In studying it, we use court, probate, death, marriage certificates, census', and other records to determine whom our ancestors were and what, when, where, and how they were born, married, and died, etc. That is how I found out about the Dudley Brothers who settled Dudleytown.

15. What is "Witches Dam", and why is it called that?

"Witches Dam" is actually Marsella Falls, located about 3/4 of the way up Dark Entry Road--it was dammed up during the heyday of Dudleytown to power a mill on Bonney Brook, the main source of water for Dudleytown. I have no explanation as to why its called "Witches Dam" other than the story that I was told about a group of Wiccans (modern day witches) who used to hold their rights a little farther down the hill.

16. What, and where, is this VORTEX?

I didn't know the answer to that one till I went there myself--and now I can tell you: The Vortex is just Cook Road (see the map). Nothing else. Cook Road was (until the fire) so grown over that it appears the trail ends about 1/4 mile down it. It really doesn't--it will continue on down the hill to another road. Because it was so grown over, its actually a more strenuous hike than Dark Entry is-- and more dangerous because of it. It gets *very* claustrophobic there, and that may account for the weird feelings some get there. CAUTION--THIS IS THE AREA OF THE RECENT FIRE--it destroyed parts of the trail, and you could become lost quickly. Since Dudleytown is now closed, this is a moot point, but should it reopen, I suggest you stay away from it for about a year till some of the foliage comes back.

17. Well, you sure give a lot of "cautions." Sounds like you're trying to cover something up!

Those who have actually been there will tell you my "cautions" are not a joke--even if they disagree with me as to wether or not it is haunted. Even some Paranormal groups will tell you that. The area IS dangerous, even by day. At night it is just *crazy* to go there. You MUST be familiar with the rules of hiking, and be appropriately dressed to attempt this trip. IF you know what you are doing, and with the necessary precautions, you will have a nice hike. Unfortunately, some of the email I get plainly show that so many city folk try this not knowing what they are doing---and some pay the price with sprained ankles, bruises, and hundreds of mosquito bites.

18. You say there were never any Ghosts, yet the Warrens, in their lectures and books, say that Dudleytown people kept seeing

"hoofed footed creatures." How do you explain that?

The Warrens are the *only* ones who have ever said that. "Creatures" and "demons" are *never* mentioned in any of the stories, books, and magazine articles before <u>Ghost Hunters</u> that I am aware of, and I have read hundreds of versions of the legend. I have no idea where their version of the legend and the background history came from. I have sent email letters to their web site, asking for sources, but received no response from them. Their book does not include a Bibliography, and therefore nothing they say can be checked. Because of this, most Paranormal Societies and Investigators that I know discount their version entirely.

19. Who are these weird people that some folks see when they go there--the ones that ask questions and all?

Probably some of the locals that are out for a hike, OR, it could be other hikers who "know" the legend and are out to scare you. As for locals, remember, they do *not* want you there. They *will* be suspicious. If they are DEF members---they are also the owners of the place! If you are treating the land with dignity, are being careful, and not responding to them with disrespect--they usually will leave you alone. Act like a bunch of "Ghostbuster" rejects and they will call the State Police. Pure and simple. However, IF you notice that your new acquaintances are *really* weird, leave and call the Police yourself. I have never heard of this being necessary, but you never know. Be aware that they could also be members of a Paranormal Group out to "investigate" the area. These folk are usually harmless--but are out for a "ghost hunt." They will find something, I am sure. They always do.

20. How long will Dudleytown remain closed?

That is hard to say. Some people are now starting to (I can't believe this) *steal* the "No Trespassing" signs, and DEF is not amused. The last I heard is that the closure is "indefinite." DEF has plans on posting new signs every fifty feet or so going up the roads that lead into Dudleytown.

One thing is for sure: the Connecticut State Police have a standing request to be out in force every Halloween.

21. Has your web site had an affect on Dudleytown? Do you think your book will?

Actually, the web site (I am proud to say) *has* had an affect. I happen to know of *many* Paranormal groups who look to it for the latest news of the area. Many "Presidents" of these groups have emailed me to thank me for the info, and I have noticed a *lot* of other web pages urging caution and respect of the property should it ever open again. Of that I am quite proud and happy. *Some web pages have actually dropped Dudleytown from their list of "haunts" and places to visit.*

Do not think, however, that the web page has changed everyone's view. While many now say there was no "curse" of the Dudley's, most still believe it is haunted. But at least it is a beginning.

As for this book–I sure hope it has an affect. Maybe at least as much as the web page. I do not harbor any hope for a miracle, however. The Legend is to widely known now. These things, I am sad to say, do not ever seem to go away.

22. You are just doing this for the money, right?

Right, and I am going to retire tomorrow! I only wish! I am a High School History Teacher who has spent about $5,000 doing the research for this book, and I only *hope* I will break even or at least get a tax break! Publishing costs are astronomical. As this book will be classed "Historical/factual," hopes for a long publishing history are slight. Sorry, but I only did this because I am interested in it, and thought others might be also.

# Appendix 1
# DUDLEYTOWN TIME LINE

This is only a quick overlook at the main events at Dudleytown. They include only the FACTS. I have included a few things about my research, etc.

**Note: Those marked with an (\*) are curse related.**

**(\*) 18 Aug 1510. Edmund Dudley is beheaded by Henry VIII. History books will record this as a "scapegoat measure."**

**24 June 1532. Robert Dudley, the Earl of Leicester, born.**

**1573 Robert Dudley, son of the Earl of Leicester, born.**

**4 September 1588. Robert Dudley, Earl of Leicester, dies of old age in England.**

**11 September 1608. William Dudley is born in Sheen, Surrey, England.**

**1639. William Dudley arrives in America aboard the ship St. John, establishes Guilford,**
**Connecticut.**

**September 1649 Robert Dudley, ONLY son of the Earl of Leicester, dies of old age in Florence,**
**Italy.**

**(\*) 31 July 1653. Governor Thomas Dudley dies in Roxbury Massachusetts of old age.**

14 September 1674. Joseph Dudley is born in Saybrook Connecticut.

1706. Gideon Dudley is born in Saybrook.

11 May 1710. Abiel Dudley is baptized in Saybrook

7 April 1725. Barzillai Dudley is baptized in Saybrook.

(*) 1739 Thomas Griffis buys land at the Cornwall Land Auction.

24 Jun 1747. Gideon Dudley buys land in Cornwall.

7 July 1748. Abiel Dudley buys land in Cornwall. Gideon Dudley arrives in Cornwall.

5 Dec 1748. Abiel sells his land to his brother Barzillai.

31 December 1748. Barzillai Dudley buys more land in Cornwall.

2 Jan 1749. Gideon Dudley, son of Gideon, born in Cornwall.

6 March 1750. Barzillai Dudley marries Sarah Carter in Cornwall.

16 May 1750. Sibe Dudley, daughter of Barzillai, is born in Cornwall.

1 February 1752. Sarah Dudley, daughter of Barzillai, is born in Cornwall.

15 February 1752. Elizabeth Dudley, daughter of Gideon, is born in Cornwall.

23 October 1753. Abiel Dudley buys more land in Cornwall, arrives sometime before 1754.

**1754. THE FRENCH INDIAN WAR BEGINS.**

14 November 1755. Joseph Dudley, son of Gideon, is born in Cornwall.

**1757. Barzillai Dudley is in Capt. Lyman's company in the French/Indian War for 14 days.**

**1758. Cornwall Tax Records reflect Barzillai Dudley for the last time. He leaves shortly**

**thereafter.**

(*) Spring 1763. The Carters move to upstate New York, at the Forks of the Delaware, and are massacred. Two daughters and a son are taken, the daughters later to be ransomed. The son will later work for the Department of Indian Affairs.

21 Jun 1763. Martin Dudley of Springfield, Massachusetts, marries Anna Dudley, daughter of Gideon Dudley, in Cornwall.

**1763. THE FRENCH INDIAN WAR ENDS.**

21 May 1765. Elisabeth Dudley, wife of Gideon, dies in Cornwall.

15 Oct 1766. Gideon Dudley, son of Gideon, dies in Cornwall.

20 November 1766. Joseph Dudley, son of Gideon, dies in Cornwall.

(*) 16 December 1771. Abiel Dudley's property sold, becomes charge of the town.

1773. Cornwall Tax Records reflects Gideon Dudley and family for the last time. He leaves shortly thereafter.

(\*)1774. Plague visits Cornwall and Dudleytown.

(\*) 1792. Gershon Hollister dies by falling during a barn raising at William Tanner's house.

(\*) November 1799. Abiel Dudley dies of old age.

(\*) April 1804. Sarah Faye Swift dies by lightning strike.

(\*) Oct 20, 1811. Mary G. Cheney is born to Silas and Polly Cheney in LITCHFIELD, Ct. She would NEVER go to Dudleytown.

5 July 1835. Mary Young Cheney marries Horace Greely. They have 5 children, but only two live.

(\* )Oct 30, 1872. Mary Cheney Greeley died of lung disease in New York City.

(\*) 1900. Dr. William Cogswell Clarke buys land in Cornwall.

(\*) 1901. John Patrick Brophy's house burns, he leaves town.

(\*) About 1917 Harriet Banks Clarke dies in New York City. Dr. Clarke marries Carita about 1919.

24 Dec 1924. The Dark Entry Forest, Inc. (DEF) is formed in Cornwall, buys 850 acres of land, including Dudleytown.

February 1926. DEF meets for the first time with 41 members. Dr. Clarke and his wife are included.

1928/29. Dr. William Cogswell Clarke is on the Board of Directors of DEF.

**1931.** An advertising pamphlet of DEF, and its "pastoral escape," The Bald Mountain Farm. The pamphlet lists Dr. Clarke, his wife, and three children as members.

**1938.** <u>They Found A Way</u> is published, the first book to speak of a curse in Dudleytown. Another book follows.

**1943.** Dr. Clarke dies of a heart attack in Cornwall Bridge.

**1970's.** All through this decade, numerous magazine and newspaper articles speak of "haunted Dudleytown."

**1988.** The Warren's book, <u>Ghost Hunters</u> is published.

**1993.** Dan Ackroyd, actor, tells "Playboy" (August, 1993) that Dudleytown "Massachusetts" is the "scariest place on earth."

**1998.** "Welcome to Dudleytown" is started as a "interesting side-page" to Gary Dudley's genealogy site...gets 200 hits the first month, over 7,000 by July 1999.

**July 1999.** "Welcome to Dudleytown" becomes its own internet site at www.geocities.com/dtownfarce, draws 300 hits its first month.

**1999.** ALL of the legend of Dudleytown is disproved. Only the "spooky story" remains.

**September 1999.** Due to vandalism, Dudleytown is closed to the public by DEF. "No trespassing" signs are posted, and 72 citations issued quickly. This situation continues to the present.

# Appendix Two
# Was there a tie between
# William of Guilford and
# Robert, Earl of Leicester?

The ongoing insistence by not only the Legend tellers, but also some historical societies and many authors, that there was a ancestral link between William of Guilford, the Dudleytown brothers progenitor to the U.S., and Robert Dudley, Earl of Leicester, has always boggled my mind. From the beginning of my genealogical research on the Dudley family, I never found one. None of the history books covering the U.S. ever mentioned one, and until I read my first "Legend" story, never had reason to believe otherwise. Dean Dudley, in the *History of the Dudley Family,* had stated that there *was* a "tradition" in the Guilford branch that it was related to Governor Thomas Dudley, but implied that there was no proof of it, and his own research contradicted the "tradition."

When I completed the research for this book, however, I had TWO possibilities of the genesis of the mistake....and mistakes they were. I will go over them as I found them.

1. As I was completing my William of Guilford book, I received an email from a young man who wanted to know if I was going to do the "traditional link through Robert Deveroux Dudley to Robert of Leicester." I was taken aback: who was Robert Deveroux Dudley? and where did this person get the information? While I waited for his answer, ANOTHER email arrived from a woman who claimed that she had a web site with much of the same information on William of Guilford as I, and would I look at her site? I did, and there it was.......William of Guilford linked to

Robert through a Robert Deveroux Dudley!

I immediately sent an email asking for her source, and the response was quick–the Whittlesey/Whittlesey Genealogy. I was just about to journey down to the library, when I noticed the mistake that was made. It was a simple oversight that was never corrected.

If you remember, Robert Dudley's second (actually third) marriage was to Letticia Knollys....the *widow of Walter Deveroux, the Earl of Essex.* Walter and Letticia had a son, named Robert. When Deveroux died, and Robert Dudley and Letticia were married, the son Robert naturally came with her. HOWEVER, please also remember that Robert *never* acknowledged the boy (or his own illegitimate son, for that matter). There is NO indication, through history, correspondence, genealogy, or anything that Robert Deveroux ever took the name Dudley. In fact, there is evidence that he did *not* take it....for HE went on to inherit his father's title Earl of Essex at age nine, and while Letticia remained his mother, he was under the care of Lord Burghley, who raised him by order of the Queen and request of his father.[103] The complications of assuming a name were enormous. Remember, the Dudley name had a serious dent in it at that time. Folks still remembered the Edmund incident, and the Lady Jane Grey usurping of the throne.

What was done was that Mr. Whittlesey *assumed* that Robert Deveroux took the Dudley surname. He was wrong. Robert Deveroux was a stepson, with denied claims to anything Dudley (including curses!).

---

[103]Weir, Alison, The Life of Elizabeth I, 1998, Ballantine Books. Page 304-305.

Case closed.

2. Right near the end of my research, I re-read a lot of my printed sources, and ran across a quote that I had not seen before (isn't that the way it always is?). In an article in "My Country" magazine, the author Brainerd T. Peck states:

> "Originally from Richmond Co., Surrey, England, William Dudley was assigned a distinguished ancestry by Dean Dudley, author of "Dudley Family," a genealogy published in 1886, which received considerable attention in earlier Dudleytown articles. Today's professional genealogists have much improved research sources at their disposal than those of a century ago and conclude that the remote Dudley pedigree offered by Dean Dudley is in need of being re-examined for confirmation and revision. This research is now under way."[104]

Mr. Peck, as one who is actively involved in "re-examining" Dean Dudley's work, I can assure you that Dean Dudley *never* assigned a "distinguished ancestry" to William Dudley. The *only* thing he said was that there was a *tradition* that the branch was related to (Governor) THOMAS Dudley,[105] and *that* was a quote from Rev. Dr. David Dudley Field. No more.

George Adlard, in his <u>Sutton-Dudley's of England and the</u>

---

[104]"Dudleytown, Cornwall's Deserted Village", by Brainerd T. Peck, in <u>My Country</u> Magazine, Vol. 22, No.2, Summer 1988, page 6.

[105]Dudley, Dean <u>History of the Dudley Family</u>, Vol 1, No.1, 1886, Salem Mass. Higgenson Books, page 96

<u>Dudley's of Massachusetts</u> postulates that the "Connecticut" (read: Guilford branch of the Dudleys) came from the Clopton house of Dudley's.[106] (see "Family behind the Legend, part 1") As I have stated in my book on the Guilford Branch, while this would be interesting (genealogically), there is no proof of it.[107]

None of the above matters, though. There is *no* link between William of Guilford and Robert, Earl of Leicester. None. What little proof that there is one turns out to be a simple mistake. Which leads us right back to the beginning.

---

[106] Adlard, George, <u>The Sutton-Dudley's of England and the Dudley's of Massachusetts</u>, 1862, reprint by Higginson Books, page 5.

[107] Dudley, Rev Gary P. <u>The New Dudley Genealogies: the Descendants of William of Guilford</u> 1999, Heritage Books, page vii.

# Appendix 3
# Doing Historical Research 101

This little appendix shows you how to do simple research. It is intended for beginners, and lists some simple steps. Do not be afraid of it–you may actually get hooked!

1. Decide on *what* you want to study, and the *time-frame* you will be working with.

For instance, with Dudleytown, I knew (from the legend) that it was founded *about* (no matter what the Warrens' said) 1747. The last incident was *about* 1920. That would be my time frame. For the moment, I disregarded the English background. I came back to that later.

2. Narrow down the *area* you will be dealing with.

For Dudleytown, I had a little work to do, for Dudleytown was on NO Connecticut maps. When I discovered that is was NOT a town, but a part of Cornwall, I narrowed my research to that. (It was only later I discovered that some of the "Legend" occurrences never happened in Cornwall/Dudleytown).

3. Go to the *Library.*

Sounds to simple to be true, but I estimate that about 50-75% of your research will be done there. Look up the State, the Town, and any historical figures you know are connected to your subject. Even if it doesn't answer any questions, you will gain a solid foundation for the rest of your research. This is where I found the Cornwall Town histories, which actually answered a great many questions about the history and occurrences at Dudleytown.

*Note: even if you believe your research will  not use genealogy, try to pick a library that has a genealogical section. My (very) large library here is San Antonio DOES have a genealogy section. The reason I state that is this: the MAIN library had NO local town histories–but the genealogical area DID. Remember that!*

### 4. Contact a *Historical Society*

Yes, I came down a little hard on the Cornwall Historical Society, but I do appreciate the help they gave me. The MAIN purpose of Historical Societies is to compile and protect the history of their designated state, town, village, etc. That is ALL they do (or should be doing), and 99% of them are *very* good at it (including, for the most part, Cornwall's). They will usually know (or know where to get) information on the history, people, and places within their domain. Most are willing to share their information, and mail or fax you what they have (either for free, or for a minimal fee). Be nice to these people, most are volunteer's and do it for either fun or a sense of obligation. Either way, they do *not* need to hear rude and immature voices on the phone! Most *will* work with you.

To see IF your selected area has one, pick up the phone and dial information and get the *area code* to your selected town. (It is VERY important to know the *modern* name for your area) IF your phone does NOT have nation wide information, then phone 1-area code-555-1212. If it does have nation wide, then just ask for the "name of town (or state, or county) Historical Society." *IF YOUR TOWN DOES NOT HAVE ONE, THEN ASK FOR THE NUMBER OF THE MAIN LIBRARY FOR THE TOWN.* You see, in may instances (and Cornwall was one of them) the Historical Society is *not* listed in the phone book, but the *Library* knew the number instead. Also, sometimes the Historical Society is either a part of, or works with, the library. I found this true in two instances during the course of this work.

Once you have the hot little number in your hand–*get your*

*ducks lined up in a row!* In other words *KNOW* what you are going to ask *BEFORE* you make your call. Even though this book was about a ghost story and other paranormal things, I assure you that most Historical Society volunteers are *not* mind readers. Do *not* waste these kind folks' time. Also, do NOT be afraid to ASK them if they can reproduce any materials they have–*but make sure to offer to compensate them.* Many times they will say their services are free–*but offer anyway.* You will find them much more willing to work with you if they know you are serious.

5. Write out what you have *found* so far.
     This is *very* important. You can not know were to go next if you do not know were you are now! List, chronologically, all the dates and instances associated with them, and what you found, then what questions you may have. (also, what conclusions you can draw from them)

     All this done, sit on your information for awhile, then go back over it.

6. *Visit*, if possible, the subject of your study.
     So much can be gained by this, that I cannot tell you the value of it. I had done 95% of my research on Dudleytown *before* I was able to go there. Once there, I inwardly got another perspective of my subject. Things just seemed to make more *sense* to me. For instance, I was so angry at DEF before I went–afterwards I completely understood their want to protect the area. Additionally, I now *understood* the trials and tribulations that living on that hill had to entail. Do it if possible.

6. *Repeat* all steps.
     Sounds like shampoo directions, doesn't it? Actually, that is all there is to it. Once you have exhausted all possible sources,

121

write it all down again. Sometimes you will see something you missed. And sometimes you will know you are done.

I have not included some of the steps I took in the process of this work, for some are a little complicated (like sorting through town vital, land, and probate records). If you are a genealogist, you know how to do this (or know were to get help with it), and can readily see how I used the additional information. The above steps, however, are simple and can solve any number of U.S. historical questions, and may open up new doors in history for you.

Enjoy!

# Index

# BIBLIOGRAPHY

So many books were consulted in writing this short tome, that it would almost take another of the same size to list them. Below are the *principal* works that were consulted.

Adlard, George, The Sutton-Dudley's of England and the Dudley's of Massachusetts, 1862, reprint by Higginson Books.

Cahill, Robert Ellis, New England's Ghostly Haunts, 1983, Chandler-Smith Publishing House.

Chamberlain, Paul H. Dudleytown, 1966, The Cornwall Historical Society.

Clark, Harriet Lydia, True Facts About Dudleytown, 1989, The Cornwall Historical Society.

Dudley, Dean, The History of the Dudley Family, 1884-1900, Dean Dudley, publisher. Now available through Higgenson Books, Salem Massachusetts

Gannett, Michael, The Distribution of the Common Land of Cornwall, Connecticut 1738-1887, 1990, The Cornwall Historical Society.

Gannett, Michael, Cornwall Documents: Town Meeting Minutes 1740-1875, 1994, The Cornwall Historical Society.

Myers, Arthur "Is the Ghost Village of Dudleytown Really Haunted?" from A Ghosthunters's Guide., 198?, Chicago, Contemporary Books.

Philips, David E. Legendary Connecticut, 1992, Curbstone Press.

Sedgwick, Charles F., General History of the Town of Sharon, 1877, Charles Walsh, Printer.

Starr, Rev Edward C. A History of Cornwall, Connecticut, 1926, Torrington, The Rainbow Press, 1982 second edition.

Sterry, Iveagh Hunt and William H. Garrigus, They Found a Way, 1938, Stephen Daye Press.

Warren, Ed and Lorraine with Robert David Chase, Ghost Hunters, 1989, St. Martins Paperbacks.

Weir, Alison, The Life of Elizabeth I, 1998, Ballantine Books.

Glenn E. White, ed., Folk Tales of Connecticut, Vol II., 1981, The Journal Press.

In addition, the Land and Vital Records of the town of Cornwall and Litchfield, Ct. were used, along with some very basic books on U.S. History for exact dates.

My sincere appreciation to Michael R. Gannett and the staff of the Cornwall Historical Society for their valuable assistance.